INTERIOR
TRANSFORMATIONS

ANN GRAFTON

INTERIOR
TRANSFORMATIONS

PHOTOGRAPHY BY SIMON UPTON

TEXT BY HELEN CHISLETT

jacqui
small

To my parents,
John and Kathleen

PUBLISHER
JACQUI SMALL
EDITOR
STUART COOPER
DESIGNER
ROBIN ROUT
STYLIST
MARY NORDEN
JANE CHURCHILL COORDINATOR
SAM WALSH
PRODUCTION
GEOFF BARLOW

THIS PAPERBACK EDITION
PUBLISHED IN 2008

FIRST PUBLISHED IN 2001
BY JACQUI SMALL,
AN IMPRINT OF AURUM PRESS LTD,
7 GREENLAND ST,
LONDON NW1 0ND
TEXT, PHOTOGRAPHY, DESIGN AND
LAYOUT COPYRIGHT
© JACQUI SMALL 2001

A CATALOGUE RECORD FOR THIS
BOOK IS AVAILABLE FROM THE
BRITISH LIBRARY.

ISBN 978 1 906417 12 3

PRINTED AND BOUND IN CHINA

CONTENTS

Introduction

The process of transforming an interior is immensely rewarding, and the effects are far-reaching. A home that is comfortable and relaxing, and that caters to all our needs, contributes much to our quality of life. Design today is about the environment we create around us and the way we live our lives. It is no longer enough to create an isolated beautiful effect

For me, the challenge of developing a new fabric is always to make sure that it will enhance the lives of our customers. As well as being aesthetically pleasing, it must also be comfortable and suitable for its purpose. I believe the same principles apply to creating a home.

Inspiration for a new fabric might come from anywhere — a wonderful scrap of antique textile, an Indian miniature painting, a piece of American folk art, or a woodland walk in autumn. Likewise the inspiration for an interior. Everything around us can be a source of ideas, from a colour in nature to an decorative chest brought back from our travels.

Translating these inspirations into reality means making myriad decisions about colours and textures, furniture and fabrics. Every aspect of a home, from the paint on the walls and the flooring material, to the way a curtain is hung or an object is placed, will contribute to its overall style and atmosphere.

The same consideration must also be given to questions of practicality and comfort. The durability of a sofa fabric, the efficiency of task lighting in a kitchen, the softness of a mattress will all have a bearing on the success of a home.

When creating my own homes, I have always tried to ensure they give me and my family pleasure while satisfying the diverse and often conflicting demands that we place on them. Our home in Cornwall, which was recently remodelled and redecorated, is a case in point. Working to a set budget and a tight schedule, the aim was to transform an unprepossessing modern house, whose main attraction was its stunning coastal views, into a welcoming, comfortable family retreat. This exercise provided a focus for the book and the results can be seen in several of the photographs.

My aim in writing this book was to guide readers through the process of transforming an interior by explaining key design principles and their effects, and by sharing some of my decorating techniques. The book can be used in a variety of ways. As well as describing how to completely transform every room in the home, it suggests simple but effective methods for revitalizing an existing scheme. These include ways of altering a room to reflect the changing seasons, which brings variety and freshness to a home, just as seasonal ingredients do to cooking. To help with decision making, the book features a range of colour palettes, fabric combinations, and interior styles.

The advice and solutions are based on my personal experience and the insights I have gained in my professional life. I hope you will be inspired to adapt the ideas, experiment with the styles and palettes, break the rules occasionally, and find the solutions that work best for you. The character of a home evolves gradually as you add layers of your own personality. What is important is that each decision you take should be an informed decision. Every home should be a considered home.

DECISIONS

FIRST THOUGHTS

It is tempting when decorating to move swiftly to the stage that people usually enjoy the most, such as choosing paints or fabrics, deciding on curtain headings or hunting for a piece of furniture. The first rule of decorating is learn to be patient. Before buying anything take a long, hard look at your home. This means looking beyond the existing decoration and furniture to assess the quality and amount of space and light, and the essential structure of walls, floors and architectural features. Only by being fully informed about your home will you be able to make the right decisions.

The space at your disposal will always be the first consideration. This is not just a question of assessing the size of a room and the height of a ceiling, but of deciding how you want to use the space and whether it will work from a practical point of view. How much natural light a room receives is crucial to making decisions, not only about the artificial lighting that is needed, but also about the colours of paint or wallpaper.

Once you have assessed the space and decided how you would like to use it, you can begin to think about the style or mood you want to create. Choosing a style can be a perplexing business but there are several techniques, such as using an inspiration board, that can help you to crystallize your ideas.

Transforming a home requires careful planning and budgeting, as well as the hiring and coordination of professionals such as builders, plumbers and electricians. You may also want to employ an interior designer to help you consolidate your own ideas or suggest new ones.

The following section will help you to think through these initial decisions and provides the skills necessary to design a decorative scheme.

ABOVE AND OPPOSITE
LEAVING A WINDOW
UNDRESSED IS AN
EXCELLENT WAY OF
GETTING TO KNOW A
SPACE. NOT ONLY WILL IT
ENABLE YOU TO ASSESS THE
AMOUNT AND QUALITY OF
NATURAL LIGHT IN THE
ROOM, BUT IT WILL GIVE
YOU TIME TO CONSIDER
THE BEST WINDOW
TREATMENT. LETTING IN
THE WORLD OUTSIDE CAN
ALSO PROVIDE VALUABLE
INSPIRATION FOR
COLOURS, TEXTURES AND
MOOD. DURING THIS
ASSESSMENT PERIOD
ONE SIMPLE OBJECT OF
BEAUTY, SUCH AS THESE
CREAMY ROSES IN A GLASS
JAR, IS THE ONLY
ADORNMENT NEEDED.

Space

The decoration of a room is a good point at which to pause and reflect on what you would like the space to offer for the next few years. Think about its purpose and whether you are making the most of it at present. Often we live somewhere so long that we take the use of a space for granted.

Function

Consider all the activities that take place in the room. A bedroom, for example, may be more than just a place to sleep. It might also be where you exercise, write letters or read. Similarly, a kitchen may be much more than a place to cook. It is as likely to be the room where the family eats or where you hold informal suppers for friends.

Changing the use of a room is often beneficial. For example, if you have a dedicated dining room that is used for Christmas lunch and about three supper parties a year, consider extending it into the living area or turning it into a study or a play room. Keep a pair of trestle tables in your attic, plus some lovely linen cloths, and you can create an impromptu dining area whenever necessary by moving furniture out of the room.

When assessing space try to imagine the walls are invisible and that each room flows into the next. This can reveal new possibilities, and you may decide to dramatically reshape your space by removing or erecting partition walls. If so, consult an architect or master builder to find out if your ideas are feasible. It is usually possible to make such changes, as long as you seek professional advice.

Dimensions

When deciding on furniture and decoration, it is important to take into account the size and shape of a room.

Small rooms have the special benefits of cosiness and intimacy, which can be emphasized through the choice of colours (see page 40) and fabrics. Flexible furniture will increase the uses of a small space – for example, a sofa bed can transform a living room into a spare bedroom when needed – and there are many imaginative ways of augmenting storage space, for instance by using drawers on casters that slide under a bed.

With small spaces, the best approach is to scale up rather than down – this applies not only to furniture, mirrors and paintings, but also to the scale of pattern on flooring, walls or fabrics. A large-scale damask wallpaper, for example, gives the impression of opening out a room and will enhance the feeling of space. The trick is to decorate a room as though it is large; then it will appear to be so.

Larger spaces and rooms that have unusual proportions – such as an L-shaped room – also need special consideration. It is often easier to divide such spaces into two or more separate areas. For example, you could incorporate two groups of seating or create areas for different activities. The division can take the form of a physical barrier, such as a screen, or simply a large piece of furniture, possibly a free-standing bookcase or a sofa. Alternatively, the areas can be defined by distinct decorative treatments, perhaps by painting walls in one area and using wallpaper in another.

Floor plans

A floor plan is invaluable for working out the best use of space in a room. Draw the plan to scale on 1 centimetre square graph paper, with, for example, a 1 centimetre square representing

BELOW WHEN CONSIDERING HOW TO DECORATE A SPACE, TAKE INTO ACCOUNT ITS RELATIONSHIP WITH ADJACENT ROOMS. THIS DINING AREA HAS AN OPEN DOORWAY THAT GIVES A VISTA TO THE LIVING ROOM BEYOND. DIFFERENT TYPES OF FLOORING DEFINE THE TWO SPACES, BUT THE SAME FAMILY OF COLOURS HAS BEEN USED TO CREATE A FEELING OF HARMONY THROUGHOUT.

OPPOSITE THE PROPORTIONS OF A ROOM SHOULD BE USED AS A GUIDE WHEN CHOOSING FURNITURE AND DETAILS. IN THIS LOW, BEAMED LIVING ROOM THE SEATING IS GENEROUSLY ROUNDED BUT NOT TOO HIGH, THEREFORE ALLOWING LIGHT FROM THE WINDOW TO STREAM IN. A HIGH-BACKED SOFA WOULD HAVE BLOCKED OUT LIGHT FROM THE WINDOW AND MADE THE SPACE APPEAR CLAUSTROPHOBIC. TALL LAMPS AND TOPIARY BUSHES ON THE WINDOWSILL ARE POSITIONED TO CREATE THE ILLUSION OF HEIGHT.

20 centimetres in reality (1:20). Measure the walls and draw the outline of the room on the plan, marking the position of doors, windows, alcoves and fixed features such as radiators and power sockets. Write the measurements around the outside of the plan for easy reference. You can then draw in the new layout for the room, including furniture, equipment such as a television, lighting, and any built-in features like cupboards and shelving. These must all be drawn to the same scale as the room.

Cutting the shapes of larger items of furniture out of coloured paper will enable you to move them around the plan to find the best position; alternatively draw different layouts on sheets of tracing paper laid over the plan.

It is also useful to draw a sketch of each wall. Mark the height and width of the wall, the position and dimensions of doors, the size and shape of windows, alcoves, fire surrounds, skirting boards and cornices, and the location of light switches and plug sockets. This will be an invaluable source of reference when choosing furniture, light fittings or new doors. It will also prove useful for estimating quantities for paint or wallpaper and curtains or blinds.

PRACTICAL SPACE PLANNING

- Place furniture to make the maximum use of natural light
- Do not block light by putting tall items in front of windows
- Place televisions and computer screens away from windows and direct sunlight to avoid poor visibility
- Work out the 'traffic flow' through the room to allow freedom of movement
- Avoid placing square or rectangular pieces of furniture at an angle in a corner as it creates dead space
- Make sure the door into the room and cupboard doors can be opened easily
- Place lamps and electrical equipment near plug sockets and away from where the cables could become hazardous; draw new sockets on the floor plan if necessary

Light

Light has a major bearing on our enjoyment of a room. Natural light contributes greatly to a sense of well-being but it is rarely enough on its own. Artificial light also has an impact on mood, and should not be regarded purely as a practical means of illumination. Both natural and artificial light affect colour (see Colour Codes, page 26), and must be taken into account when choosing the decoration for a room.

Natural light

There are several factors to consider with natural light. First, decide if there is sufficient light in the room for its intended use. For example, if the kitchen is to be the hub of the household, at all hours of the day, at all times of year, then it should ideally be a room with a generous amount of natural light. Owners of period homes often move the kitchen because when such houses were built, it was frequently located in a dark, gloomy place. By comparison, drawing rooms were often on the first floor of large town houses where they would enjoy the benefit of excellent natural light.

Consider also how light changes during the day and how it falls in different areas of the room. Dark corners may need a subtle boost of artificial light. Conversely, a wall that floods with light can provide the inspiration for a bold colour treatment. Look at the patterns that light creates as it comes into the space and decide if these can be emphasized through the choice of window treatment.

It is also important to be aware of how light changes through the seasons. This may determine how rooms are used during winter and summer and will reveal at what times of year you need to maximize natural light and augment it with artificial light. Light is one of the key considerations if you want to alter the decorative scheme according to the season (see Timely Changes, pages 164–165).

Finally, consider how the light is affected by the external environment. Rooms that look out on fields have quite a different feeling to those overlooking city walls. A sense of location is key.

If the amount of natural light is not compatible with how you want to use the room, you have two options: to explore ways of bringing in more natural light, perhaps by adding another window or changing solid doors to glass ones; or to boost existing daylight with artificial light.

Artificial light

There are three main types of artificial light. Task lighting relates to an activity such as reading or preparing food; suitable fittings include overhead or wall-mounted spotlights. Ambient lighting is used for creating mood; examples are floor-standing uplighters or lamps.

Display lighting is used to highlight an object or to illuminate a painting; the latter is achieved with special picture lights, for instance.

Some lights combine several functions. For example, table lamps are useful task lights and they lend atmosphere to a room; spotlights can be used for either task or display lighting as needed.

One of the most versatile and easily installed lighting features is a dimmer switch, which will give you the option of instantly changing from bright illumination to subtle mood lighting as the occasion demands.

Most rooms will need a mixture of task and ambient lighting, and of overhead and lower-level lights. Avoid too much bright overhead light as this will not create a relaxing atmosphere. Essentially you should aim to create several layers of light in each room: the more layers, the more ways there are of lighting the space – and so of changing activity and mood.

As well as deciding what types of lighting are required, it is also important to ensure that the lights themselves suit the style of the room. (The decorative uses of lights are covered in Style Makers, page 183.)

Last but not least are the practicalities. Decide whether the room requires additional sockets for table or floor lamps, or whether cabling needs to be installed for wall lights. Such tasks should be carried out by an electrician *before* you decorate.

ABOVE LEFT THE PALETTE OF FRESH BLUES, WHITES AND CREAMS IN THIS SEASIDE LIVING ROOM HAS BEEN CHOSEN TO TAKE FULL ADVANTAGE OF THE BRIGHT NATURAL LIGHT.

OPPOSITE THE TABLE IN THIS DINING ROOM IS PLACED TO MAXIMIZE NATURAL LIGHT. THE WINDOWS HAVE BEEN LEFT UNDRESSED SO DINERS CAN ENJOY UNINTERRUPTED VIEWS.

Style and Mood

Choosing a style and mood for a room is one of the most enjoyable aspects of decorating. It is also one of the most important – what you choose will inform all your decisions about colours, textures, flooring materials, fabrics, furniture and decorative details.

Finding a personal style

You may already have a strong sense of the right style for your home and may indeed have chosen the property for this reason – be it an Arts and Crafts house in the country, an apartment in a Georgian town house, or a clapboard cottage by the seaside. This, in turn, may dictate your choice of colours – either historical or modern – as well as the design of your furniture. However, you could of course choose to disregard the historical provenance of your property, as discussed below under 'Architectural style'.

The inspirations for interiors can be many and varied. Travel, for instance, has a strong influence today, as do references from museums or art galleries. Interiors magazines and books on every subject from decorative tiles to Indian palaces offer a wealth of inspiration, as does nature, from the colour of autumn leaves to the texture of bark. Inspiration can also come from a single object you either own or would like to acquire. An oriental rug or a painting, for example, can suggest the colour scheme for an entire room.

Take the time to research these and other sources of ideas, and to evolve your own personal style. Decide on the foundation for each room – the colours and textures you would like to use and the major items of furniture – and gradually add in the other elements: the textiles, paintings and decorative objects.

If you have to design a room with a partner who has opposing views – traditional versus contemporary, for example – it is important to begin by creating a neutral backdrop. You can then add elements that will appeal to both parties, such as a modern piece of furniture or paintings from both traditional and modern schools, thus creating an eclectic and interesting home.

Architectural style

When choosing a decorative style consider the architectural style of the room. Look at such features as cornices, skirting boards, fireplaces, dados, doors and windows and decide if they are compatible with what you would like to achieve.

Architectural features can be either accentuated or moderated, depending on the effect you want to create. However, it is important not to feel constrained by them. Unless you live in a listed building, such features can be replaced or removed. For example, picture rails are sometimes better taken down if they are not used. This will enable you to take paper or paint from floor to ceiling in an unbroken line to create an impression of height in the room. An unattractive fireplace might be better removed to make room for a bookcase or an additional sofa.

Well-defined cornices and skirting boards give character to a space. The continuing popularity of the Victorian terraced town house proves that such period detail is classic enough to move with the times. Behind the facade of traditional houses often lie the most wonderful modern interiors.

Remember, though, that whereas period homes lend themselves to contemporary treatments, most modern homes do not benefit from a historical approach. Modern architecture is usually defined by the cleanness of the line, and faux traditional architraving, for example, simply looks wrong. Take inspiration from the graphic qualities of such designs – at times they almost dictate what is to be done. This applies not only to colours and patterns but also to shapes and forms. Such messages can provide a welcome starting point for a scheme.

OPPOSITE THE COLOUR INSPIRATION FOR THIS COMFORTABLE LIVING ROOM – A BLEND OF NEUTRALS, BLUES AND TERRACOTTAS – CAME FROM THE PAINTING THAT HANGS OVER THE FIREPLACE (SEE PAGE 20 FOR A CLOSE-UP VIEW). WHEN DECORATING, IT OFTEN HELPS TO FIND A STARTING POINT LIKE THIS, BE IT A RUG, A DECORATIVE OBJECT OR A WORK OF ART.

Mood

When people think about the effect they want to create in their homes, what they are often considering is mood or atmosphere: whether a room is to have a sense of being relaxed or formal, stimulating or calming, cool and airy or warm and cosy. Whereas style is mainly about putting a look together, mood relates to how you want to feel when in a room. The two concepts are closely related and the style you choose for an interior will have a strong influence on its atmosphere. Is your living room to be relaxed and eclectic or ordered and elegant? Do you favour a kitchen that is high tech and efficient or should it be a more leisurely space where papers are read and the radio enjoyed?

If a space has several functions, such as a living room that includes a play area or a home office that converts to a guest bedroom, it may be necessary to alter the mood according to who is using the room and at which time of day. (See Timely Changes, pages 166–167.)

Light and colour have a strong impact on mood. Put very simply, subdued lights are relaxing and bright lights are stimulating. Similarly, soft creams and quiet taupes send out very different signals to hot reds and rich greens.

Texture is also important. Consider fabrics, for example: a room decorated with simple cottons and lightweight sheers is very different in character from one dominated by chenilles and velvets. The same is true of surface materials: a wooden floor provides a different atmosphere to a thick wool carpet, just as a stripped-pine table has a character quite unlike an antique mahogany one.

As with choosing a style, recall the interiors you have enjoyed being in. They may be rooms you remember from your childhood, rooms in friends' homes, or interiors you have visited while travelling. Think about why they left such an impression on you. Was it the colour scheme, the floor treatment, the furniture, the lighting, or a combination of several factors? Consider how you can translate the elements you liked into your own home to create the desired atmosphere. Study photographs in books and magazines of rooms you feel particularly drawn towards, and analyse what you like about them. Then make a list of the features that all these interiors have in common. This exercise should provide you with the starting point for an inspiration board.

THIS WATERCOLOUR OF A MOROCCAN MARKET SCENE WAS THE INSPIRATION FOR THE SEASIDE LIVING ROOM SHOWN ON PAGE 19. IT IS THE ANCHOR PIECE FOR BOTH SUMMER AND WINTER SCHEMES, COMBINING AS IT DOES SOFT AQUAS AND CREAMS WITH EARTHY TERRACOTTAS AND TAUPES. BEING A WATERCOLOUR, ITS EFFECT CAN ALTER SLIGHTLY ACCORDING TO LIGHT – JUST AS THE COLOURS OF A ROOM DO WHEN THE SEASONS CHANGE.

Using an inspiration board

This is an invaluable tool for designing a decorative scheme, and should ideally be completed before making any purchases. To create the board all you need is a large, sturdy piece of white cardboard. Gather tear sheets from magazines, fabric swatches and colour inspirations, and keep them in a suitable box. As you begin to develop your ideas for the room, attach these items to the board using double-sided tape. Buy paint sample pots so you can apply patches of the colours to the board. Add the paint colours and fabric samples in roughly the same proportions as they will be used in the room; use small pieces of fabric for cushions and larger pieces for sofas, curtains and floor coverings. The board should contain all the main items to be used in the room, and could include photographs of existing features and sketches of new ones. On the reverse of the board write the contact details of suppliers and the product references. Keep the inspiration board when you have finished decorating as it will be invaluable if you need to match or replace any of the elements at a later date.

THE INSPIRATION BOARD FOR THE
WINTER SCHEME OF THE LIVING
ROOM ON PAGE 19 FEATURED
NEUTRAL PAINT COLOURS FOR THE
WALLS AND A WARM PALETTE OF
NATURAL FABRICS, INCLUDING
PLAIN AND CHECK TERRACOTTA
CHENILLES AND WOOL FELT. THE
BOARD INCLUDED PHOTOGRAPHS
SHOWING THE ORIGINAL ROOM AND
FIREPLACE AND IDEAS FOR NEW
LIGHTING. SKETCHES WERE USED
TO VISUALIZE FURNITURE SHAPES,
UPHOLSTERY TREATMENTS, AND A
NEW DESIGN FOR THE FIREPLACE.

Planning

Whether you are transforming a whole house or a single room, it is important to spend some time on planning the work and setting a realistic budget. In the long term, it will help you to avoid making costly mistakes.

Organizing the work

Good planning means organizing the work logically and allowing sufficient time for each task. On the page opposite is a checklist of the key tasks involved in transforming a room, in a suggested order in which they could be completed. Adapt this to suit your own needs so you have a list of everything that has to be done. Add estimated times where appropriate so you can coordinate the

different aspects of the work and any professionals you need to hire. It is important to be aware of the chain reaction between one decorating task and the next. For example, if the painter falls behind schedule it will have a knock-on effect to the carpet fitter. If a task cannot be carried out when originally planned, you will need to revise the timing of that task and any later work that it affects. Even the best-laid plans can sometimes go wrong and a flexible approach is essential.

Employing help

If you want to do your own decorating, most tasks are relatively straightforward so long as you use the right equipment, work safely and learn a few basic techniques. Any electrical or plumbing work should be carried out by professionals. If you are planning to make structural changes, such as knocking down or building walls, it is essential to consult a master builder or an architect on the feasibility of your plans and to have them implemented by reputable builders.

Others whose skill and experience you may need to call upon include decorators, curtain makers, upholsterers, carpet fitters, flooring specialists, and furniture and cabinet makers. If you are having a new bathroom or kitchen fitted or a complicated lighting system installed, it is best to go to a specialist firm that can advise on design and materials as well as carrying out the work.

When choosing contractors there is no better recommendation than word of mouth. If this is not possible, ask prospective contractors if you can contact one or two previous clients to enquire about the service they received. Find out if the work was carried out to a good standard and to the agreed schedule and budget. Once you have chosen someone, ask them to provide a detailed quotation, including the cost of materials and labour, the schedule and the payment terms. With expensive structural work it is worth getting two or three contractors to quote so you can compare prices. However, it is important not to base your decision on cost alone.

Consider also employing an interior designer, who will work with you to bring your ideas to fruition. A good designer will analyse your likes and dislikes, your lifestyle and your budget, and devise effective solutions. A designer can also save you time and effort by taking responsibility for hiring other professionals and coordinating the project.

Interior designers operate on different levels: some will advise on the complete restructuring of an interior; others are more involved with decisions about colour and fabrics. Designers have a large database and are able to source a wide range of materials that you may not have the time or knowledge to locate.

As with contractors, it is worth trying to use a designer who is personally recommended. If this is not feasible, look at the work of designers in interiors magazines or contact a professional body and request a list of members. Try to see several designers initially. Ask them about the range of work they carry out and study portfolios of their recent commissions. Once you have narrowed the candidates down to those whose work and approach you like, ask them to provide itemized quotations and fee proposals.

Setting a budget

Working out a budget will help you to plan realistically and to control costs. Begin by compiling three lists. The first should comprise essential items such as structural changes, alterations to services such as electricity and plumbing, the installation of items such as bathrooms and kitchens, and major decoration. The second list should focus on key pieces of furniture such as sofas, beds, tables and chairs, as well as window treatments, storage, and fixed lighting. The third list should include accessories like cushions, throws, upholstery trims, mirrors, pictures, lamps and objects – items that add the important finish to a room.

Now assess the items you already own and on each of the three lists include the things you would like to keep or would be prepared to live with until your budget allows or you find the ideal replacement.

When you have compiled the three lists, estimate how much money you will need for the new items on each one. Be as detailed and as specific as possible in your estimates, and where appropriate budget for the best quality you can afford. Remember also to add in the cost of any professional help needed. When you arrive at your total figure, it is wise to add at least 10 per cent extra to cover any unforeseen expenditure that may be necessary.

If you find it difficult to finalize all the costs at the beginning, or you think you may run over budget, be realistic and change your plans. Review your choices but try not to economize on items where quality is essential. Be prepared also to reconsider your overall design – you may end up with an alternative you prefer. It is also important to establish your priorities. For example, you may decide to spend a large proportion of your budget on a new kitchen and delay a bathroom until a later date. Remember that the best homes are not completed in a week; they evolve over time.

CHECKLIST OF DECORATING TASKS

Planning Assess space and and light and decide if any structural changes are needed for intended use > Decide what professional help is needed and get quotes > Draw floor plans (see page 14) > Decide on decorative scheme, furniture (including built-in) and lighting > Work out quantities of materials and buy or order them > Order made-to-measure fabrics such as curtains or blinds and upholstery

Structural changes Remove any unwanted walls or erect new ones > Install new services such as cabling, electrical fittings and plumbing > Strip off any old wallpaper and repair plaster, or replaster if necessary (allow plenty of time for drying) > Lay hard flooring such as tiles or woodstrip > Repair or install detailing such as skirting boards and cornices > Hang new doors and repair or replace window frames and glazing > Install any built-in furniture > Connect radiators, sinks, etc. to plumbing

Decorating Apply undercoat or lining paper to walls and ceiling > Add final paint finish or hang paper (start with ceiling and work downwards) > Fix light switch and socket plates > Attach curtain poles or rails > Lay carpet or other floor covering > Hang curtains or blinds > Attach light fittings > Install fixed shelving > Place furniture in position and fit any loose covers > Put up pictures and mirrors and position ornaments

ABOVE CHOOSING A NEUTRAL FOUNDATION FOR WALLS, FLOOR AND FURNITURE WILL ENABLE YOU TO CHANGE THE STYLE OF THE ROOM MORE EASILY IN THE FUTURE.

OPPOSITE WHEN WORKING TO A BUDGET IT IS IMPORTANT TO BE AWARE OF ALL THE DECORATIVE OPTIONS. YOU MAY BE ABLE TO KEEP AN EXISTING PIECE OF FURNITURE, SUCH AS A SOFA, BUT USE LOOSE COVERS TO GIVE IT A FRESH LOOK.

COLOUR CODES

When people think about decorating, what they are often visualizing is colour. The thought of a 'blue room' or a 'red room' is very powerful and evokes all sorts of images – not just of the room itself, but of how it is going to be used and its atmosphere.

Although a room might be described in terms of a single dominant colour, most rooms contain several shades. Usually, a base colour is applied to walls, floor or furniture and corresponding hues are introduced in the form of curtains, floor coverings, textiles and objects, so creating a blue room with white and yellow, or a red room with green and black. In this way, the foundation colour is diluted and blended, resulting in a more harmonious effect.

We are drawn towards certain colours not just because they fit in with a particular style of decorating, but because of their psychological effect. In simple terms, white is calming and red is stimulating, blue is cool and yellow is happy, but this is only part of the story. Our reaction to colour is also highly subjective and is often rooted deep in our pasts.

Inspiration for colours to use in our homes can come from anywhere. They might be shades that occur in nature, such as the colour of pebbles on a beach or a garden flower, or hues that are present in a favourite object, such as a painting or a piece of blue-and-white china. Gather textiles, objects, tear sheets from magazines, flowers and anything else with colours that appeal to you and study them carefully; you will probably discover that certain shades or combinations occur repeatedly.

Deciding which colours you like is a vital part of decorating. However, it is equally important to understand how to use and combine these colours to create particular moods and effects. This chapter explains how to harness the power of colour to transform your home.

THIS PAGE AND OPPOSITE THE NATURAL WORLD IS A RICH SOURCE OF INSPIRATION FOR COLOURS AND COMBINATIONS OF COLOURS. THE MORE YOU LOOK AT A PIECE OF ROCK OR A PLANT, THE MORE COLOURS YOU WILL SEE. AT FIRST GLANCE, THE WREATH OF SEASIDE PEBBLES SHOWN OPPOSITE MAY APPEAR WHITE, BUT LOOK MORE CLOSELY AND YOU WILL FIND SHADES OF GREY, OATMEAL, BLACK AND BROWN. SIMILARLY, WE DESCRIBE THE SKY AS 'BLUE', BUT AS THE SEQUENCE PICTURED LEFT PROVES, IT CAN CHANGE FROM CORNFLOWER BLUE TO DENIM TO INDIGO TO SLATE GREY WITHIN MINUTES. AS IT DOES SO, THE CHANGING LIGHT ALTERS THE WHOLE LANDSCAPE.

Understanding Colour

Colour is one of the most uplifting and evocative ingredients you can bring into your home. To use colour well it is necessary to understand how it is affected by both natural and artificial light, how different colours work together, and how colour influences mood.

Colour and light

The importance of assessing natural light when deciding on the use of a space was discussed earlier. It is also vital when choosing a colour scheme, because light can either bring a colour to life or deaden it.

First be aware of the type of natural light coming into the room. The colder the light, the better suited it is to slightly warmer colours – cream as opposed to brilliant white; terracotta rather than orange; aquamarine instead of turquoise. Secondly, observe how external factors affect the light in the room. The light in a built-up area is filtered and flattened, and is quite different to that found in wide open spaces.

Remember that light changes throughout the day and from season to season. If a room receives sun only in the mornings and this diminishes during the winter, do not make the mistake of decorating it as though it were a sunny room. Opt instead for a scheme that can be easily adapted to the changing seasons by the use of loose covers, throws, cushions and rugs (see Seasonal Changes, pages 162–165).

The amount of light a room receives also has a profound effect upon colour. It is tempting to paint a dark area brilliant white, but this will only make it look dingy. Work with the character of a room rather than trying to force a colour scheme upon it. Dark rooms look magnificent painted in rich shades such as mushroom or vermilion red. For rooms used mainly in the evening or in winter, such as formal dining rooms or cosy living rooms, these dramatic colours are ideal.

Consider also the effect of artificial light on colour. In rooms with only one overhead lighting source the light becomes diffused and the colours become dull. It is therefore best to create a layered scheme, including uplighters that can be used to wash a wall with light or spotlights that highlight key features. The choice of bulbs and shades is also important. Halogen bulbs produce a clear white light that has the least discernible effect on colour. However, unless it is diffused or reflected, halogen light is too bright for rooms intended for relaxing. Here the warmer glow of tungsten bulbs is more comfortable although it will not render colours as accurately.

OPPOSITE
HALF-GLAZED DOORS
AND SHEER CURTAINS
ALLOW LIGHT TO POUR
INTO THIS COTTAGE
LIVING ROOM. SOFT
GREENS AND PINKS
MAKE A PRETTY
COMBINATION, WITH
AN ACCENT COLOUR OF
RASPBERRY ON THE
CHAIR COVER TO ADD
A SHARPER NOTE.
BLEACHED BARE BOARDS
IN THE SUMMER ARE THE
PERFECT WAY TO
EMPHASIZE THE LIGHT,
AIRY FEEL OF THE ROOM.
NOTE HOW FEW
COLOURS HAVE BEEN
USED TO BUILD UP THIS
EFFECT: WALLS AND
FLOOR ARE VERY
QUIET, BUT THE PINK
CHECK INTRODUCES
VITALITY AND INTEREST.
REPLACING THE
CURTAINS WITH
SOMETHING THICKER,
AND DARKER IN THE
WINTER, SUCH AS A
TERRACOTTA CHENILLE,
WOULD GIVE A QUITE
DIFFERENT LOOK
TO THE ROOM.

Work with the character of a room rather than trying to force a colour scheme upon it.

Colour and mood

Colour is a powerful tool for creating mood, whether it is the purity of whites, the calm of earth tones, the freshness of greens and yellows or the opulence of deep reds and aubergines. Of course, it is not just a simple matter of using one colour to create an atmosphere but of selecting a palette or family of colours for the feeling you want, and using these in varying proportions for the different surfaces and elements in the room.

It is important to choose the right shade of a colour for the effect desired. For example, not all blues are 'cool'. A blue with lots of magenta is in fact a warm colour. Similarly, greens can be as fresh as iced peppermint tea or as enveloping as a pine forest.

Make sure too that the atmosphere of a room reflects its use. For instance, in a room intended for relaxation the colours should be calm and harmonious.

Choosing colours

It makes sense to choose colours carefully and to try them out in a room before making a commitment. First, find the samples you like. When looking at paint charts, bear in mind that our opinion of a colour can change when we are surrounded by it. A colour in a two centimetre square may seem acceptable, but when it is magnified to the scale of a room it may be too strong. As well as ordering a sample of the shade you chose first, try one that is two tones paler.

If you want to match a colour to an element in the room, carry a sample of it on your shopping trips. If this is not possible, take an item with a similar colour but make sure it has the same texture as well, because materials absorb light in different ways.

Once you have made your choice, take a metre square of MDF and cover it with the proposed paper or paint (if using paint, apply the correct undercoat first). Now stand it in the room and go in to look at it through the day and evening, in natural and artificial light. Move it around from wall to wall as some areas receive less light than others. Note how the colour becomes flatter or more vibrant according to the time of day, and consider if this suits the use of the room and the mood you want to create.

OPPOSITE THIS LIVING ROOM ILLUSTRATES THE IMPORTANCE OF ACCENT COLOURS. DECORATED IN HARMONIOUS BLUES AND GREENS, THE ROOM HAS BEEN GIVEN A VISUAL LIFT WITH THE ADDITION OF THE RED SIDE TABLE. THE COLOUR IS PICKED UP IN THE CUSHION AND FLOWERS.

ABOVE THE PIMENTO RED OF THE RATTAN SIDE TABLE FROM THE ROOM SHOWN OPPOSITE IS A WONDERFULLY VIBRANT COLOUR. SMALL PATCHES OF RED HAVE A STIMULATING EFFECT, PARTICULARLY IN AN OTHERWISE NEUTRAL ROOM.

When looking at paint charts, bear in mind that our opinion of a colour can change when we are surrounded by it.

A room that has blue walls and white doors
and architraving is very different in character
from a white-painted room with blue detailing.

Combining Colours

Combining colours is not difficult provided you learn a few basic principles. As with any other decorative technique, it is best to begin simply, with some tried and tested combinations. Later on, as your understanding of colour grows, you may want to add a few twists of your own, or try out some more unconventional schemes.

It is worth remembering that everything you put into a room has a colour of some sort and so provides a way of layering the overall effect. As well as using the major elements – surfaces, fabrics, furniture and floor coverings – you can employ less obvious items such as lamps, books, flowers, pictures and frames. Look round the room you are sitting in now – you will probably be surprised at how many colours there are.

Key words when using colour

When working out colour schemes the key words to remember are base, tone and accent.

The base colour is that which is used in the greatest proportions, usually the wall shade. Often it is chosen because it provides the perfect canvas on which to use other colours.

Tone relates to the darkness or lightness of a colour. Two different colours that have the same tonal value or depth will work in harmony. Soft aquas, dove greys and powder pinks go well together, for example, but change the pale pink to fuchsia and you have a contrast. If you want to keep an equilibrium, concentrate on using colours that tone well.

Accent colours are contrasting shades that are used in small amounts to introduce a visual jolt into a scheme. Think of a blue living room

with orange cushions, for instance, or a soft green kitchen with hot pink china. Adding or changing accent colours, in the form of textiles, ceramics, lamps, objects and flowers, is an effective way of introducing fashionable colours or of breathing new life into an interior scheme (see A Touch of Colour, pages 174–177).

Colour proportions

As is clear from the discussion of key words, combining colours effectively also means thinking about the proportions in which they are used. For example, you might like the idea of a room that is decorated in blue and white. But is it going to be a white room with blue or a blue room with white? The answer usually lies in the colour of the walls, because this is the largest area in the room. A room that has blue walls and white doors and architraving is very different in character from a white-painted room with blue detailing. If you are uncertain about using strong colour, go for the latter option: neutral walls with highlights of colour. This will give you the chance to live with a shade before making a big commitment to it.

Simple colour schemes

An easy way to begin using colour is to limit yourself to just three shades. For example, if you like calm schemes, try using three neutrals together. In a warm-toned room, this might mean white with cream and a touch of yellow. In a cool-toned room, it could be white with grey and taupe.

BELOW YELLOW HAS BEEN USED AS
A SUNNY HIGHLIGHT COLOUR IN
THIS COMPACT BEDROOM. WHERE
SHUTTERS HAVE BEEN CHOSEN IN
PLACE OF CURTAINS OR BLINDS, IT
MAKES SENSE TO GIVE THEM MORE
IMPACT BY PAINTING THEM IN A
STRONGER SHADE THAN THE
WINDOW FRAME. THE BOLDLY
PATTERNED BEDSPREAD ANCHORS
THE TWO MAIN COLOURS
TOGETHER AND IMPRINTS
CHARACTER UPON THE ROOM.

The three-colour method can be used for almost
any palette. First choose a neutral from the white to cream
spectrum, possibly to use on the woodwork. Then add the
colour that will be most evident in the room – the base
colour – perhaps for the walls, window treatments or
upholstery. This could be soft blue. Finally, add an accent
colour, which is strong but will be used in much smaller
proportions; primrose, say, for cushions, throws, vases or
trims on upholstery or window treatments. Numerous
combinations can be created with this formula. What it
demonstrates is that almost any colour can be combined
with any other, so long as vivid colours are used in much
smaller amounts than the more subdued ones.

Another simple option is to
choose different tones of one
colour. A blue scheme can be
created using the spectrum from
aqua to navy, or a green one that
ranges from sage to emerald. Again,
unless you want a dramatic effect,
use the strongest colours in the
smallest amounts.

Tricks with colour

Colour can visually alter the size
and shape of a room. Cool colours –
those that contain more blue than
red – make walls appear to recede.
Warm colours – those with more
red than blue – appear to bring
walls in. If you want to include a
warm colour in a small room, avoid
using it in too solid a way. Wallpaper
and specialist paint effects are often
designed to give the illusion of
looking through to solid colour
beyond, which makes them less
oppressive in modest spaces.

OPPOSITE THIS ROMANTIC,
PASTORAL BEDROOM FEATURES THE
REVERSE COMBINATION TO THE ONE
SHOWN ABOVE: YELLOW PAINTED
WALLS HAVE BEEN HIGHLIGHTED
WITH A POWDER-BLUE BEDSPREAD
AND PILLOWCASES. AN ACCENT
SHADE OF STRONGER BLUE HAS
BEEN USED ON THE CURTAIN
HEADING AND LAMPSHADE TRIM.
THE RESULT IS A MORE
STIMULATING, LESS PLACID
ENVIRONMENT – THE PERFECT
WAKE-UP SPACE.

Just as walls can be made to
recede, so can ceilings. Painting a ceiling a lighter colour
than the walls will make it appear higher. Conversely, painting
a ceiling in a darker colour than the walls or continuing the
ceiling colour to picture-rail height will lower it visually. A
feature or area that you want to be noticed, such as an
alcove with a display of prints, can be painted in a stronger
tone than the rest of the room to draw the eye towards it.

Finally, colour can be used to influence how we feel
when we move between rooms or look from one room into
the next. To create a feeling of continuity, choose colours
that harmonize. (Using pale colours throughout will have
the effect of making your home seem larger.) For a dramatic
transition, change from calm colours to rich, dark ones.

Almost any colour can be used with any other,
so long as vivid colours are used in much
smaller amounts than the more subdued ones.

Colour Palettes

The secret of using colour successfully lies in recognizing the palette or range of palettes that best suit you and your home. Colour palettes hold no mystery: they are simply collections of shades that share the same tonal values and therefore work well together.

Over the next few pages you will find six examples that not only combine well visually, but also imprint a certain mood upon a room. They are named according to the atmosphere they evoke – Calm, Sunny, Cosy and so on – and may help you to decide how a particular room should feel. For example, you might want to create a feeling of calmness in a bedroom or cosiness in a living room.

Colours can appear in more than one palette. Sage green, for example, occurs in both Sunny and Cosy, and grey appears in Calm and Smart. What matters is their juxtaposition with other colours to produce a particular look and atmosphere.

These are all tried and tested combinations that will guarantee success, but they are by no means the only permutations possible. Use them as a catalyst to create your own colour palettes.

Calm

In an increasingly hectic world it is no surprise that many people are seeking sanctuary in neutral colour schemes. These encompass a whole range of whites and creams, and an infinite variety of oatmeals, greys, taupes and browns. Colours are often borrowed from nature, so think of chalky cliffs and pebble beaches or wheat fields against grey skies and you begin to see how much scope they offer. Neutral palettes are the most adaptable and work well in any area to bring a sense of calm.

Seaside

Shades inspired by the seaside are fresh and invigorating. Blue is a key player here and can range from the grey-blue of winter seas to the clear blue of summer ones. Think also of all the shades from dark blue-green to the palest of aquas. Be aware of the textural dimension when working with this palette – often colours are not solid, but have a distressed finish. They look best in airy rooms with warm light as they can veer towards the 'cold'. If this is a concern, use patches of pimento red with blue, or soft pink with aqua, to bring warmth to the scheme. Crisp cottons or linens, faded denims, every scale of gingham and large chequerboard patterns all suit this palette.

Sunny
If you want to use warm, happy colours, consider the Sunny shades. Yellows of all hues, from the palest primrose to the deepest egg yolk; yellow mixed with white and the softest of creams; cobalt blue and sage green all combine to give the impression of a bright, sun-filled interior, even on the dullest of days. Using the stronger tones in this palette will create a vibrant scheme. Alternatively, use the paler colours, such as sandy yellow or apple green, in copious amounts. Introduce highlights to Sunny schemes using the deeper or brighter shades for blankets, vases, glasses or even trimmings on cushions. Sunny colours translate marvellously into patterns such as checks, stripes and florals, which when combined will create a wonderful patchwork of colour.

Pretty If there is one word that sums up the Pretty palette, it is pink. The pink of sunrises, of roses and of strawberries with cream. Pink's usual partner is green in all its many shades, being reminiscent of summer gardens where other pretty colours, such as yellows and peaches, also reside. Hot pinks can be used to create a decadent atmosphere, while other shades of pink can transport us back to a gentler era – think of sprigged cotton, Regency stripes or rose-covered chintzes. Team them with buttery yellows, soft greens and milky whites for a romantic look that is perfect for anything from a bedroom to a breakfast room, a living room to a bathroom. Florals should always be evident as they are synonymous with the comfortable atmosphere Pretty colours provide.

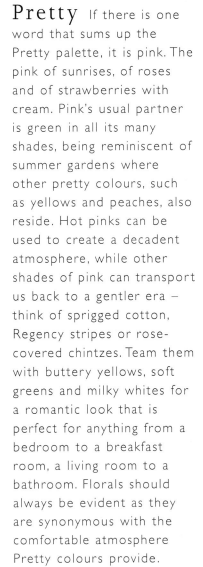

Cosy

In rooms where you want to feel colour wrapped around you for comfort, use the autumnal tones of russet, mole, clay, ochre, terracotta and the rich greens of fir trees. These are earthy, country colours, used to bring warmth into a room. Combine them with the gentle colours of heather such as pale mauve and soft sage green, and include natural colours of oatmeal, straw and linen. Red tones, such as claret and the more purplish bordeaux, add richness to this palette. Cosy colours combine well when the same tonal values are used. These shades have a timeless quality that makes them an excellent choice for period homes. They are often seen in fabrics that provide warmth and texture, such as wools, velvets, felts, printed fabrics and heavy natural linens.

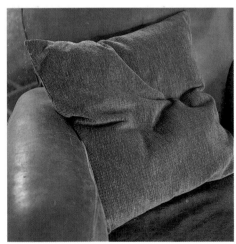

Smart With colours including navy blue, black, greys, hot reds, such as crimson and pimento, and all shades of white and cream, the Smart palette suits a graphic, tailored look. These colours can be used in different combinations according to the location. In rural homes, perhaps with natural or painted floors, navy blue and hot reds work well. Suitable fabrics include ticking stripes, checks in all sizes, sailcloths, coloured linens and all weights of cotton. In city homes navy blue is often replaced by black or slate grey, which is combined with dove grey and highlighted by reds, oranges or terracotta. More graphic patterns, such as large-scale checks and bold stripes, work well in a city environment. Whatever combination you choose, soften the stronger colours with whites and creams.

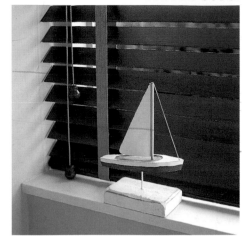

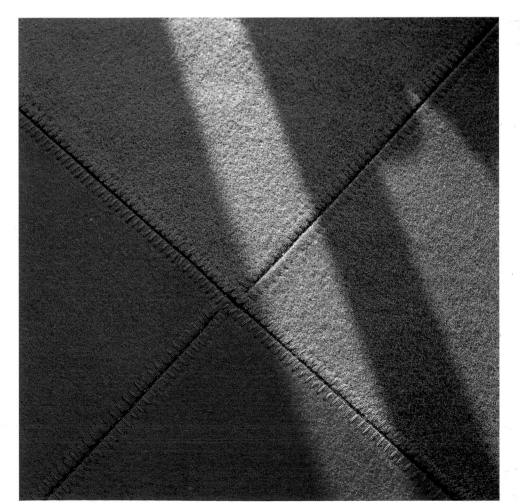

DECORATION

SURFACE
ATTENTIONS

Walls, floors and ceilings are the large planes of a room. Because of their dominating proportions, they must be considered with care. Each must be thought about not only individually but in relation to the entire room. Together these surfaces form the canvas on which to introduce other colours, patterns and textures.

The decisions you take regarding these surfaces relate back to your initial thoughts about the room: how you want to use it; the quality and amount of space and light, and the style and colours you favour (see Decisions, pages 10–41). Another key factor is the budget: whereas painted walls and ceilings are relatively inexpensive to alter, a floor is a costly item to change.

In simple terms, the main decision to be made about surfaces is whether to draw attention to them or use them as a backdrop. This in turn will determine how decorative they should be. The amount of colour or pattern you introduce onto each one will have a direct influence on the complexity of the decorative scheme. If in doubt, keep surfaces as plain and as neutral as possible: there will be plenty of scope to introduce layers of decoration later through the use of furniture, textiles, lighting and accessories.

Doors, windows, skirting boards, cornices and fixtures such as radiators must be considered in conjunction with these large expanses. Although they are proportionally smaller, they play a vital role in defining the perimeters of the room. Regard them as visual punctuation, places where the eye pauses to consider the effect as a whole.

ABOVE COVERING A SURFACE IN A BOLD PATTERN, SUCH AS THE MOIRÉ CHECK OF THIS FABRIC WALLING, GIVES A ROOM CHARACTER AND VITALITY. IT IS PARTICULARLY EFFECTIVE IF YOU WANT TO DRAW ATTENTION AWAY FROM CRAMPED DIMENSIONS OR UNINTERESTING ARCHITECTURE, CREATING INSTEAD AN OASIS OF TEXTURE AND COLOUR.

OPPOSITE COMBINATIONS OF FLOORING – HARD WITH SOFT, PLAIN WITH PATTERNED – ARE OFTEN THE MOST EYE-CATCHING WAY OF TACKLING A FLOOR AREA. THEY NOT ONLY OFFER THE FLEXIBILITY TO ALTER THE LOOK OF A SPACE ACCORDING TO WINTER AND SUMMER TEMPERATURES, BUT ARE A WAY OF LAYERING A SCHEME THROUGH COLOUR AND PATTERN. HERE, SANDED BOARDS PROVIDE AN ATTRACTIVE AND PRACTICAL BASE, WHILE THE WOOLLEN RUG BRINGS A TEXTURAL DIMENSION TO THE ROOM. THE BOLD SQUARES REFLECT THE PATTERN ON THE CUSHIONS, BUT THE INCREASED SCALE ADDS ANOTHER POINT OF CONTRAST.

ABOVE IN A SCHEME THAT IS BASED ON NEUTRAL
COLOURS AND PLAIN TEXTURES, IT MAKES SENSE TO
PAINT OR PAPER WALLS IN CALM, HARMONIOUS
TONES. THIS CREATES A QUIET BACKDROP FOR KEY
PIECES OF FURNITURE.

OPPOSITE IF YOU HAVE A GROUP OF PAINTINGS,
CHOOSE A WALL COLOUR THAT WILL MAKE A SUITABLE
BACKDROP. THE FOREST GREEN USED HERE HAS
DENSITY WITHOUT BEING DOMINANT. THE CREAM
DADO PROVIDES CONTRAST AND PREVENTS THE
SCHEME FROM BEING OVERWHELMING. THE DADO RAIL
AND SKIRTING BOARD HAVE BEEN PAINTED TO MATCH,
SO THE EYE IS NOT DISTRACTED FROM THE PRINTS.

BELOW THE FABRIC WALLING SHOWN IN CLOSE-UP ON
PAGE 45 IS SEEN HERE IN SITU WITHIN A CITY DINING
ROOM. BECAUSE IT IS SO STRONG, THE OTHER COLOURS
IN THE ROOM – IN PARTICULAR THE UPHOLSTERY AND
TABLECLOTH – HAVE BEEN KEPT NEUTRAL.

Walls

The key to choosing wall decoration is to think beyond the wall
being simply a boundary. It might, for example, provide a visual link
between one room and the next or a backdrop to a focal point
within the room.

Choosing wall coverings

When choosing wall coverings, decide whether you want the walls to
recede into the background or whether they should have more impact
in the scheme. This will guide you towards neutrals and plain colours
on the one hand or patterns and stronger colours on the other.

It is also important to consider what will go against the wall.
If you have paintings, objects and imposing pieces of furniture, they
must sit comfortably with the wall colour. For example, rich wooden
antiques, decorative collections and traditional oil or watercolour
paintings can look effective against deep, strong colours. Think of the
forest greens and vermilion reds that are found in some art galleries.
You will also need to decide how to light such pieces and whether
to install picture lights or other fittings before decorating.

Pieces with a more textural beauty – such as shells or a
collection of fossils – can be placed against a pale, slightly distressed
surface to bring out their aesthetic qualities.

If what is going on or against the walls is not an issue, the
decorative treatment comes back to personal preference: paint or
paper, colour or neutral, smooth or textured.

Some homes have beautifully textured walls such as stone or
rough plaster, which can be further enhanced through colour or
lighting. Conversely, if a room has few interesting features, consider
covering the walls with pattern for character or a strong texture,
such as hessian. Or opt for fabric walling, such as a moiré check, to
provide a sense of luxury and warmth.

If you have inherited someone else's decorating tastes and
are not sure what to do, the best option is to paint the walls white.
Choose a shade of white that is soft rather than brilliant – one third
of magnolia mixed with two thirds of white is an excellent way of
achieving a more muted effect. With so many shades of white now
available, you can even choose three shades of white for the same
room, subtly altering the tone and texture.

Living with this bare canvas for a while will give you a greater
insight into the room's good and bad points, while also allowing you
to observe the amount and direction of natural light. Colour can be
added through furniture, textiles, paintings and decorative objects.
Once you understand the room better, inspiration for stronger
colours or bolder patterns may follow more easily.

It doesn't matter whether you want to use paint, wallpaper
or fabric for your walls, the important thing is to take the largest
sample possible and live with it for a while before making a decision
(see Colour Codes, page 28). This applies to white paint as well as
colours: a white paint can appear pinker, yellower or greyer according
to where it is used in the room.

If you have paintings, ornaments and imposing pieces of furniture, they must sit comfortably with the wall colour.

ABOVE TONGUE-AND-GROOVE PANELLING HAS
PRACTICAL ADVANTAGES AS WELL AS
AESTHETIC APPEAL. IT CAN BE USED TO
CONCEAL UNEVEN OR UNSIGHTLY WALLS, IS
ABLE TO WITHSTAND HEAT AND STEAM, AND,
IF FITTED AND TREATED CORRECTLY, WILL
LAST A LONG TIME. SYNONYMOUS WITH
RUSTIC SIMPLICITY, TONGUE-AND-GROOVE
PROVIDES THE IDEAL BACKDROP FOR SHAKER-
STYLE FURNITURE AND ACCESSORIES, SUCH
AS THIS PEG BOARD. IT CAN BE PAINTED IN
ANY COLOUR, WHICH MEANS DECORATIVE
SCHEMES ARE EASILY CHANGED.

BELOW THERE IS OFTEN GOOD REASON TO
LEAVE SURFACES UNCHANGED. THE WALLS OF
THIS OLD FARMHOUSE ARE BEAUTIFULLY
DISTRESSED WITH AGE, SO THE ROUGH
PLASTER AND PITTED SURFACE HAVE BEEN
LEFT TO BECOME A FEATURE.

Practical considerations

In certain areas, such as hallways, kitchens, bathrooms and children's rooms, the durability of wall coverings is important. Some vinyl wallpapers are now virtually indistinguishable from regular papers. Like paint, they are highly practical and can be an asset in family homes.

Always consider maintenance when choosing a wall covering: will you be able to wash or renew it on a regular basis? A dado rail, with a hard-wearing surface below, and a more decorative treatment above, is a good way of combining practicality with aesthetics.

If you are using wallpaper, buy at least one spare roll from the same batch in case repairs are necessary. This is important not only because the pattern may be discontinued, but because colours from different batches will vary. Wallpaper can be difficult to hang, so consider hiring a decorator to do it for you. It is also best to seek professional advice if you are planning to install fabric walling.

Architectural features

Architectural features can either be a prominent part of the decorative scheme or play a more passive role. If you choose the latter option the conventional treatment is to paint door frames, window frames and skirting boards white or off-white depending on the colour scheme. Use eggshell or flat oil paint rather than gloss as it gives a softer look to the room but still offers a level of sheen.

If the room has unattractive features, such as the skirting boards often seen in modern houses, consider painting them the same colour as the walls. This will not only 'remove' them but also create the feeling of height in the room.

If you do not want to disguise these features, they can be used to add colour and contrast to an interior. For example, in a child's bedroom a scheme could be designed with yellow walls and blue window frames and skirting boards. In areas of heavy use, such as halls, it may be practical to paint skirting a darker colour; black or dark grey looks smart. Window frames also look impressive in darker colours, particularly if they do not have curtains or blinds, such as a window on a stairway. If you want to paint plain panel doors the same colour as walls, consider using a contrasting colour on the door frames and skirting. Painting door and window frames the same colour as the skirting boards helps to unify a scheme. To define these features while ensuring they harmonize with the walls, paint them two shades darker than the wall colour. Give architectural features as much thought as the rest of the scheme.

LEFT BORDERS BETWEEN WALLS AND CEILING ARE AN EFFECTIVE WAY OF MAKING A ROOM APPEAR BETTER PROPORTIONED, PARTICULARLY IF A GEOMETRIC PATTERN IS USED. THIS BLUE-AND-WHITE CHECK IS DEEP ENOUGH TO VISUALLY LOWER THE CEILING, MAKING THE SMALL BATHROOM APPEAR SQUARER THAN IT IS. CHECKS BESTOW A DISTINCTIVE CHARACTER ON A ROOM, ONE THAT IS SIMPLE YET ELEGANT, MODERN YET TIMELESS. USING THE PATTERN ON THE SOAP BAG UNIFIES THE SCHEME.

LEFT TONGUE-AND-GROOVE PANELLING CAN ALSO BE USED TO CREATE A DADO, AS IN THIS COUNTRY BEDROOM. IF YOU ARE DESIGNING ONE YOURSELF, BEAR IN MIND THAT HEIGHT IS IMPORTANT – THIS ONE HAS THE CORRECT PROPORTIONS FOR THE ROOM, WITH ITS TALL CEILING AND LONG WINDOWS. THE VERTICAL PLANKS EMPHASIZE THESE FEATURES. DADOS CAN BE USED EITHER TO SEPARATE A PLAIN AREA FROM A PATTERNED ONE OR, AS IN THIS ROOM, TO INTRODUCE A TWO-TONE SCHEME.

RIGHT WHEN DECIDING ON A WALL COLOUR, CONSIDER THE FURNITURE THAT WILL BE PLACED AGAINST IT, AND HOW THIS MIGHT VARY FROM WINTER TO SUMMER. THE PALE OCHRE OF THESE WALLS MAKES A GOOD FOUNDATION FOR THE RICH, EARTHY SHADES OF UPHOLSTERY AND CUSHIONS. BOLD PATTERN HAS BEEN USED, BUT IN SMALL PROPORTIONS SO THAT IT DOES NOT DOMINATE THE ROOM.

LEFT WALLPAPER BRINGS COLOUR, PATTERN AND SCALE TO A ROOM. HOWEVER, IT IS MORE DIFFICULT TO CHANGE THAN PAINT, SO CHOOSE A DESIGN YOU WILL NOT TIRE OF QUICKLY. THE BOLD WALLPAPER SHOWN HERE ENVELOPS THIS MASTER BEDROOM, MAKING IT UNNECESSARY TO HANG ANYTHING ELSE ON THE WALLS.

Doors

When thinking about door treatments, first decide how decorative you want the door to be in the scheme. If you are lucky enough to have a beautiful old door with antique door furniture, it is worth making a feature of it.

The most obvious way of drawing attention to a door is to paint it in contrasting shades to the rest of the room, perhaps using a second shade on the panels, if it has them. A more ordinary door can be either replaced, customized or made to blend in with the rest of the room. To make a door blend in, simply paint it the same colour as the walls or two shades lighter or darker.

Consider also how 'solid' the door should be and whether it should block out a view of an adjacent space or give a glimpse into it. Stable doors between a kitchen and garden are good if you have young children, because they allow light and fresh air in while also letting you keep a watchful eye on what is happening outside.

Glass-panelled doors allow you to 'borrow' light from outside or from the room next door. If you do not want a clear view through, choose plain frosted or etched glass, which has the same effect but is only translucent. Walls that have several solid doors, such as

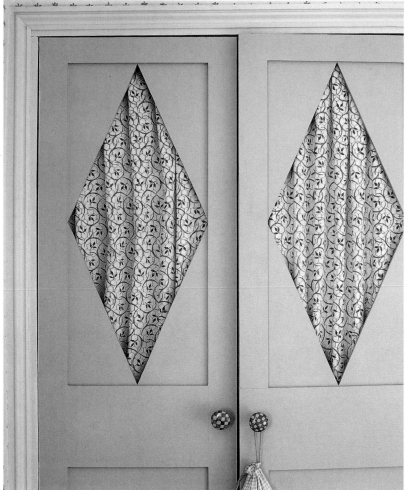

kitchen cupboards or fitted wardrobes in a bedroom, can be rather claustrophobic, so consider exchanging panels for glass or even using tightly meshed chicken wire to give a more airy effect.

Cut-outs are a fun way of customizing doors, particularly for children's rooms. These can be simple shapes, such as hearts or diamonds, or can take on more complicated forms such as favourite animals. Stencilling on doors can also create a decorative effect, whether it is a motif echoed from elsewhere in the scheme or a calligraphic device, such as a child's name.

Finally, give thought to the door furniture – handles, fingerplates and so on. These should be in keeping with the room's style, be it period or modern, simple or decorative. Replacing the door furniture is one of the easiest ways of revitalizing a room.

ABOVE BRING NEW LIFE TO OLD CUPBOARD DOORS BY HAVING SHAPES CUT OUT OF THE FRAMES, SUCH AS THE DIAMONDS SHOWN HERE. HANGING FABRIC BEHIND THEM GIVES A SOFTER LOOK TO A BEDROOM.

LEFT THE SIMPLEST IDEAS ARE OFTEN THE MOST EFFECTIVE. THIS EXTRA-WIDE FARMHOUSE DOOR HAS BEEN LEFT IN PLACE, BUT THE CALLIGRAPHIC LETTERING GIVES IT A MODERN TWIST. YOU CAN APPLY THIS TECHNIQUE ANYWHERE IN THE HOME, BUT CHILDREN IN PARTICULAR WILL LOVE IT.

Ceilings

As with doors, think about how much attention you want the ceiling to have. Architectural features such as cornices or a ceiling rose can be either emphasized or moderated. Similarly, a beamed ceiling can become a focal point of the room or its impact can be reduced by painting beams and plaster in matching white or cream.

Think too about the effect of light fittings. An elaborate chandelier will draw the eye upwards, while tiny spotlights set into the ceiling have less visual impact. Special features such as ceiling fans not only provide ventilation, but create interesting shadows, which in turn make the ceiling a focus of interest.

People usually give far less attention to ceilings than they do to walls, but the ceiling colour has a marked effect on the proportions of a room. A ceiling that is darker than the walls will appear lower, while a paler ceiling will appear higher. If in doubt, paint the ceiling white, but if you want to be a little more adventurous, try picking out the cornice in a darker colour.

If there is no cornice, consider how to make a neat break between the walls and the ceiling. Wallpaper borders, used either with paint or with a coordinating

wallpaper design, are an effective way of solving this problem. It is also perfectly acceptable to continue wallpaper over the ceiling. In fact, if you are using a highly patterned design, such as toile de Jouy, this is to be recommended, as the idea is to achieve a room in which you are enveloped by pattern. It also makes practical sense in a room in which it is difficult to define where the wall ends and the ceiling begins, such as an attic bedroom or a bathroom that is tucked under the eaves.

Ceilings in bedrooms tend to be noticed more than in other rooms, which provides an opportunity to make them more decorative. One option is to use patterned wallpaper, for example a star motif. Children may also appreciate some form of decoration on their bedroom ceilings.

ABOVE JUST AS THE DISTRESSED SURFACE OF WALLS CAN ADD TO THE CHARACTER OF A HOME, SO CAN THAT OF CEILINGS. THE PLAIN JOISTS AND UNPLASTERED TIMBER SHOWN HERE ARE PART OF THE CHARM OF THIS RUSTIC BUILDING.

LEFT CORNICES ARE THE TRADITIONAL WAY OF MARKING WHERE CEILING AND WALLS MEET. IF YOU ARE LUCKY ENOUGH TO HAVE ORIGINAL CORNICES, LIKE THIS HANDSOME EXAMPLE, MAKE A FEATURE OF THEM BY PICKING THEM OUT IN A DIFFERENT COLOUR.

RIGHT FLOORBOARDS ARE
TOUGH AND WARM AND CAN BE
VARNISHED OR PAINTED IN ANY
COLOUR. IN SUMMER, THEY GIVE
A COOL, AIRY FEEL TO A ROOM
WHILE IN WINTER THEY CAN BE
DRESSED WITH RUGS FOR A
COSIER LOOK. SAND THEM WELL
TO PREVENT SPLINTERS, AND
TREAT THEM AS THE OBJECTS OF
BEAUTY THEY OFTEN ARE.

OPPOSITE PAINTING A PATTERN
ONTO BOARDS CREATES A NEW
LOOK FOR A FLOOR. HERE
GEOMETRIC SQUARES ADD
INTEREST TO THE FLOOR OF A
BREAKFAST ROOM, THE ONLY
PATTERN IN AN OTHERWISE
NEUTRAL SCHEME. WHEN
UNDERTAKING SUCH PROJECTS,
IT IS IMPORTANT TO PLAN THE
PATTERN SO IT FITS ACCURATELY
WITHIN THE FLOOR AREA.

ABOVE THIS OVERHEAD VIEW OF
THE FLOOR SHOWN OPPOSITE
REVEALS THAT THE LINES OF THE
BOARDS ARE STILL VISIBLE UNDER
THE SOFTLY PAINTED SQUARES.
PERFECTION IS NOT NECESSARY
TO ACHIEVE THE ILLUSION. SEAL
FLOOR PAINT WITH VARNISH TO
PROTECT THE PATTERN.

Floors

A floor adds comfort, colour and texture to an interior. Being such a large surface, it also has a major influence on the room's style and atmosphere. Of all the large surfaces in a home, the floor is the one with which we have most physical contact, so practicality is a key consideration.

Whatever type of flooring you favour, the golden rule is to buy the best you can afford. Floors are both expensive and inconvenient to replace, so you must be confident that they will last a long time. This applies not only to the material you choose – be it wood or stone, carpet or seagrass – but to its fitting. Never economize when it comes to employing a fitter, as their professionalism will help ensure that the floor lasts as long as possible. Regular maintenance will also add to its longevity.

Suitable flooring

When choosing flooring, first decide which materials will suit the way the room is used.

Halls and stairways are areas of especially heavy use and require tough, durable materials that can withstand a daily battering. Wood or a hard-wearing carpet is ideal in these locations.

Kitchen floors need to be durable and easy to clean so choose surfaces such as tiles, stone, varnished wood or good-quality vinyl.

In bathrooms the flooring must be able to withstand the effects of water and steam. Hard tiles are practical but if you would prefer something warmer and softer, consider good-quality vinyl or a natural floor covering such as bamboo or seagrass.

Striking the right balance between practicality and comfort is the key to choosing a floor. It is particularly important in living rooms, which are used for such a wide range of activities. Wall-to-wall wool carpet is luxurious, warm and quiet, but it may not be the most practical option. One solution is to introduce two levels of flooring: a foundation floor, such as wood, that is exceptionally durable; and a second layer, for example a rug or an unfitted carpet, which is both comfortable and colourful. This second layer of flooring will also help to moderate the noise associated with wooden floors, which can be a particular problem in a busy household.

Another advantage of using this combination of flooring is that it will enable you to alter a room

Striking the right balance between practicality and comfort is the key to choosing a floor.

season by season, simply by removing the top layer for the summer and replacing it again in the winter. Alternatively, you could change the top layer to suit the season, using a creamy cotton rug for summer, perhaps, and a richly coloured wool one in winter.

Decorative impact

Think about how much impact you want the floor to have. As with walls and ceilings, a calm, neutral floor colour will recede and become a backdrop. A highly visible floor, such as parquet or patterned carpet, imprints a bold character onto a room, while bare boards give a sense

of openness. A general rule is that the floor colour should always be darker than that of the ceiling.

The simplest option is to buy natural-coloured flooring, be it wood, tiles, stone or carpet, and then to add colour and pattern with rugs. This is because neutrals never date: if you want to redecorate in four or five years' time, it will not be necessary to change the flooring. With carpet remember that although strong colours such as dark blue can look very smart, they will show every speck of dirt.

Rugs can be changed every few years and are a way of introducing a fashion element into

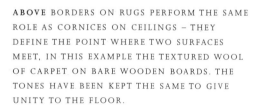

ABOVE THE DISTRESSED SURFACE OF OLD FLAGSTONE FLOORING IS ALMOST IMPOSSIBLE TO REPLICATE, SO VALUE IT RATHER THAN SEEK TO REPLACE IT. NOT ONLY DOES STONE LIKE THIS HAVE THE MOST SUBTLE ARRAY OF COLOURS, BUT IT BRINGS TEXTURE AND CHARACTER TO A ROOM. STONE FLOORS ARE WONDERFUL TO WALK ON WHEN IT IS HOT OUTSIDE AND YOU LONG FOR SOMETHING COOL UNDERFOOT; IN THE WINTER YOU CAN USE RUNNERS AND RUGS TO GIVE THEM A DIFFERENT LOOK ALTOGETHER.

ABOVE BORDERS ON RUGS PERFORM THE SAME ROLE AS CORNICES ON CEILINGS – THEY DEFINE THE POINT WHERE TWO SURFACES MEET, IN THIS EXAMPLE THE TEXTURED WOOL OF CARPET ON BARE WOODEN BOARDS. THE TONES HAVE BEEN KEPT THE SAME TO GIVE UNITY TO THE FLOOR.

RIGHT BRICK OR STONE FLOORS ARE IDEAL FOR AREAS OF HEAVY USE, SUCH AS KITCHENS OR HALLWAYS. NOT ONLY ARE THEY IMMENSELY TOUGH AND DURABLE, BUT THEY HAVE A TEXTURAL BEAUTY WHICH IMPROVES – RATHER THAN FADES – WITH AGE.

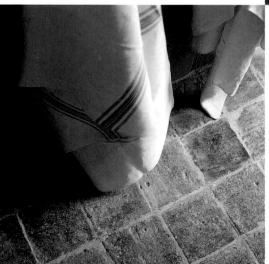

ABOVE FLOORING CAN BE USED TO MARK WHERE ONE AREA ENDS AND ANOTHER BEGINS. IT IS UNUSUAL TO COMBINE THREE TYPES, BUT HERE THE WOODEN BOARDS OF A LIVING ROOM MEET THE BRICK FLOORING OF A KITCHEN. SEAGRASS MATTING OVER THE BOARDS PROVIDES TEXTURAL CONTRAST AND ADDS FURTHER WARMTH TO THE SCHEME. WHEN LAYING FLOORS, CONSIDER HOW THEY WORK WITH EACH OTHER. COLOURS AND TEXTURES CAN BE USED EITHER TO SEPARATE ROOMS OR GIVE THEM A SENSE OF UNITY.

a room. Available in many colours and patterns, some also offer combinations of texture, such as linen with seagrass or felt with wool. Specialist carpet shops will order customized rugs containing mixtures of two or three colours or textures.

There are many ways of introducing a more individual look to a floor. Sanded wooden floorboards are a practical and inexpensive alternative to carpet, but they can be made more decorative with a stencilled or painted border or all-over pattern. Similarly, the edges of stairs, at each side of the carpet runners, can be painted or stencilled

with a decorative theme. Floor tiles offer a wide range of design possibilities, in terms of laying patterns, colour combinations, decorative borders and unusual shapes.

Consider also the relationship between different floors within your home. To create a feeling of unity, lay the same type of flooring throughout. Conversely, you can accentuate the boundaries of a room by using different styles, colours and textures of floor. In a room with distinct functions, such as a kitchen that doubles as a dining area, flooring can be used to define each area, perhaps with a tiled floor for the kitchen and a wooden floor under the dining table.

ABOVE IF YOU FAVOUR THE DECORATIVE LOOK, DON'T HOLD BACK WHERE THE FLOOR IS CONCERNED – A HIGHLY PATTERNED CARPET IS ONE OF THE MOST EFFECTIVE WAYS OF INTRODUCING COLOUR AND TEXTURE IN BOLD QUANTITIES. A PATTERN SUCH AS THIS SIGNIFIES WARMTH AND COMFORT, SO USE IT AS THE STARTING POINT FOR THE REST OF THE SCHEME. NOTE, FOR EXAMPLE, HOW THE CHAIR COLOUR AND UPHOLSTERY BRINGS OUT THE RICHNESS OF THE YARN.

ABOVE BECAUSE A FLOOR IS SUCH A LARGE SURFACE, IT CAN BE ONE OF THE MOST STRIKING WAYS OF BRINGING COLOUR TO A ROOM. FITTED CARPET OR PAINTED BOARDS ARE THE MOST OBVIOUS WAYS OF DOING THIS. THE STRONG BLUE OF THE FLOOR IN THIS NURSERY IS A DOMINANT INGREDIENT OF THE SCHEME AND SETS THE TONE FOR THE REST OF THE ROOM. OTHER SHADES OF BLUE – HIGHLIGHTED WITH PINK – ADD FURTHER LAYERS OF COLOUR.

ABOVE THERE IS A BEWILDERING CHOICE OF FLOORS AVAILABLE, INCLUDING MANY CERAMIC AND VINYL DESIGNS IN A WHOLE SPECTRUM OF COLOURS. DECIDE IF YOU WANT PEOPLE TO NOTICE THE FLOOR, OR IF IT SHOULD MERGE IMPERCEPTIBLY WITH THE REST OF THE ROOM, AS HERE.

LEFT THE SEAGRASS IN THIS ELEGANT LIVING ROOM COMBINES WITH THE WALLS TO CREATE A HARMONIOUS CANVAS, WHILE SOFT FURNISHING DETAILS ARE INSPIRED BY THE COLOURS OF THE CARPET.

MATERIAL LIFE

Fabric signifies comfort in a home. Next to colour, it also sends out the strongest messages about the style and atmosphere of an interior. Imagine a room with biscuit-coloured carpet and white painted walls. Into this space you introduce soft chenilles, warm tartans and mohair throws. This will create a very relaxed, cosy environment. Now take the same room and imagine instead smart ticking-stripe fabric, lightweight cottons and linens. This room will be much crisper and cooler.

Exploiting the chameleon quality of fabric in this way is simpler if you keep the walls and flooring fairly neutral. That way you can introduce a new look for the summer or winter by changing curtains, loose covers, cushions and throws.

The choice of fabrics today is immense. Not only is there a fabulous range of classic weaves to explore – including cottons, chenilles, linens and velvets – but technological advances have made it possible to include many more, for example Alcantara, which is a faux suede. Materials such as embroideries, denim, mohair and cashmere have moved out of the fashion world and into the home. Printed textiles, from romantic florals to whimsical designs, classic toile de Jouy to elegant damasks, are now available in an amazing array of cloths, including lightweight chintz, linen, silk and velvet.

Remember too that fabric is not limited to upholstery and curtains, but encompasses table linen, cushions, throws, blinds, lampshades, bed linen, upholstered headboards, trimmings, tie-backs, upholstery piping and decorative framed textiles. This breadth of choice gives plenty of scope to be bold and creative within any decorative scheme.

When choosing fabrics, it is important to think about them in terms of both visual and physical comfort. This chapter explains how to select fabrics for every kind of decorative purpose, and shows how to use them successfully.

OPPOSITE ONE RECENT TREND IN THE INTERIORS WORLD HAS BEEN THE RENAISSANCE OF TEXTURED DESIGNS. THESE NOT ONLY ENCOMPASS MATERIALS SUCH AS SUEDE, CHENILLE, VELVET AND SHEERS, BUT INCLUDE THE EMBELLISHMENT OF PLAIN FABRICS WITH EMBROIDERY. THE BAY TREE MOTIF SHOWN HERE IS EMBROIDERED ONTO WHITE COTTON, WHICH GIVES IT A HOMELY LOOK.

ABOVE THE IDEA OF MIXING OLD FABRICS WITH NEW IS ALSO BECOMING INCREASINGLY POPULAR. THE COTTON TRELLIS QUILT ON TOP OF THIS BED IS BORDERED WITH AN ANTIQUE FLORAL DESIGN. THIS IS A CLEVER WAY OF MAKING AN OLD REMNANT GO FURTHER: IF YOU DON'T HAVE ENOUGH TO MAKE A COMPLETE ITEM, USE IT AS A TRIM ON SOMETHING ELSE. THE BLUE WOOL BLANKET AND WHITE LINEN VALANCE ADD TEXTURAL CONTRAST, WHILE ECHOING THE SAME COLOURS.

Choosing Fabrics

Which fabrics you choose relates to the key issues of suitability, style and mood, and budget.

Suitability

Fabrics must always suit the function of a room. Materials used in an area that suffers a lot of wear and tear, such as a family room, need to be more durable than those in a guest bedroom. Although fabrics can be treated with protective sprays, it does not mean they will stay looking pristine if subjected to boisterous children or animals. Pale-coloured fabrics or expensive cashmere cushions would obviously be inappropriate for this scenario.

Comfort is of paramount importance when choosing upholstery fabrics. Hard-wearing materials such as chenilles, wools, cotton ottoman or linen union with some nylon for added strength are ideal as they are both soft and durable.

Loose covers are practical and are invaluable if you intend to change the look of a room according to season. They can be used not just for major pieces such as sofas and armchairs, but for dining chairs and upholstered headboards. Use a fabric that can be easily washed or dry cleaned, such as cotton. Loose covers should be precisely that: loose. It is generally best to use heavier-weight or stiffer fabrics such as velvets, chenilles and taffetas for tight fitted upholstery and to use lighter-weight, softer fabrics such as cotton or linen to make loose covers. These lighter-weight fabrics are also usually easier to clean.

When combining fabrics in the same item, for example when making a linen tablecloth with a wool border, it is worth collecting a mixture of samples in neutral colours and differing weights and textures. Place them together and consider only their tactile qualities. This will help you to determine from a practical point of view which mixture of fabrics is best for the intended use, before getting involved in the details of colour, pattern and scale.

Suitability also comes into the choice of window treatments. If the room is to be used frequently during winter evenings, heavy curtains will be needed to keep out cold draughts. In a more summery space, choose a voile or lightweight cotton. Privacy is another practical consideration. In a town or city, half shutters, cafe curtains, sheers or blinds will keep prying eyes out, while allowing light in. These can be combined with dress curtains for a more formal look.

Consider also the colour fastness of curtain fabrics. Even in a cool northern climate, fabrics that are subjected to strong sunlight will eventually fade. In recent years, there has been a vogue for using unusual fabrics as inexpensive curtains, such as block-printed designs from Africa or Indian sari fabrics. These look fabulous, but vegetable dyes fade quickly if exposed to bright sun. Silk is not recommended in hot, sunny climates as it will rot.

ABOVE LEFT COTTON, VOILE AND LINEN MAKE A WONDERFUL COMBINATION AS THEY ARE BOTH SOFT AND NATURAL – THE IDEAL CHOICE FOR THE WINDOW IN THIS UNCONTRIVED ROOM. RATHER THAN BEING USED TO EDGE THE SIDES OF THE CURTAINS, WHICH WOULD HAVE CREATED A MORE FORMAL LOOK, THE LINEN FORMS HORIZONTAL BORDERS AS WELL AS COVERING THE BOTTOM SEAM. THE EFFECT IS QUIETLY SOPHISTICATED, BRINGING JUST ENOUGH INTEREST TO THE SCHEME.

ABOVE RIGHT HERE A NATURAL LINEN CURTAIN HAS BEEN COMPLEMENTED BY A COTTON AND LINEN TASSEL. ONE OF THE PLEASURES OF USING LINEN IS THAT IT SUITS SO MANY STYLES OF ROOM: LINED LINEN CURTAINS WITH FORMAL HEADINGS CAN LOOK VERY SMART, WHILE UNLINED ONES LIKE THIS SUIT THE SIMPLEST OF INTERIORS. THE TIE-BACK IS DESIGNED SO THAT THE CURTAINS ARE SWEPT BACK IN A WAY THAT IS NOT TOO STRUCTURED.

BELOW LEFT WHEN CONSIDERING WINDOW TREATMENTS, REMEMBER THAT IT IS NOT NECESSARY TO USE CURTAIN FABRIC. ANY LENGTH OF FABRIC, FROM A SARI TO A SHEET, CAN BE TRANSFORMED INTO AN ELEGANT WINDOW DRESSING. IN THIS COSY LIVING ROOM, A PLAIN WOOLLEN BLANKET MAKES THE IDEAL CURTAIN FOR WINTER. IN SUMMER IT CAN BE REPLACED BY SOMETHING LIGHTER AND AIRIER, SUCH AS MUSLIN. THE TIE-BACK IS MADE OF PLAITED JUTE, WHICH COMPLEMENTS THE NATURAL TEXTURE OF THE WOOL.

BELOW RIGHT A CHECKED WOOL BLANKET HAS ALSO BEEN USED TO DRESS THIS WINDOW SET INTO THE EAVES. BY PULLING AND GATHERING THE THREADS AT THE TOP AND SIDES, A FRINGE HAS BEEN MADE, WHICH GIVES IT A SLIGHTLY MORE DECORATIVE LOOK. IF YOU HAVE AN UNUSUALLY SHAPED WINDOW SUCH AS THIS, REMEMBER THAT YOU DO NOT HAVE TO HANG THE CURTAIN AGAINST THE WINDOW BUT CAN POSITION IT TO FORM A DRAUGHTPROOF SCREEN FROM THE REST OF THE ROOM.

Style and mood

Fabrics play a key role in defining the style and mood of a room. Every fabric has four main elements – colour, texture, scale and pattern – and each of these contributes to a room's character.

Colour is the most powerful element and most people are aware of how certain colours make them feel (see pages 26–28). Texture has an enormous influence on atmosphere: rich velvets, silks, tapestries and organza bring a feeling of opulence and grandeur to a room, whereas antique linens, block-printed fabrics from Asia and simple cotton checks create a feeling of simplicity and relaxation. Patterns are often directly related to a certain look: a riot of roses, for example, is synonymous with English romance just as a thin stripe adds a smart edge. Scale also plays a part – a large-scale design brings an air of confidence to a room, while scaled-down patterns are often perfect for rooms where a calm atmosphere is desired, such as a child's nursery.

Once you become aware of the effects of these different elements, you will find it much easier to choose the appropriate fabrics for your own home.

Budget

After you have thought about the issues of style and suitability, consider your budget. Be realistic about what you can afford and purchase wisely. This means taking the time to research major items such as sofas and curtains and thinking twice before buying on impulse or purchasing items in a sale. Rather than trying to compromise all round, it is often better to make one or two items look terrific and find cost-effective solutions in other areas. For example, you might decide to choose luxurious fabrics for your furniture and a smart but inexpensive window treatment.

For major pieces such as sofas and armchairs choose upholstery that is timeless. You can always add cushions or loose covers to introduce fashionable colours. If the fabric you would like to buy for a sofa or armchair is currently beyond your budget, you could leave it in calico cotton for a while.

Remember that even a small amount of a luxurious fabric can be effective. Covering an ottoman, a large footstool or a pair of occasional chairs with silk, velvet or a highly decorative print will make a strong visual impact in a room.

Another way of extending a budget is to use two different fabrics for the same item. Traditionally, chairs were often upholstered with an expensive cloth at the front and a less expensive cotton or ticking stripe at the back. This will also add interest to the piece and is a clever method of combining an old fabric with a new one.

Window treatments are another area where a budget can seem to disappear quickly. Many shops sell simple, inexpensive blinds or plain cream ready-made curtains that will provide an effective solution until your budget allows you to be more ambitious. Remember that the best homes evolve over time.

ABOVE LEFT THIS COMFORTABLE ARMCHAIR IS UPHOLSTERED IN NATURAL LINEN, BUT IN WINTER AN ANTIQUE CHEQUERBOARD WOOL BLANKET IS THROWN OVER IT FOR ADDED COSINESS. THE CUSHION IS MADE OF BLEACHED WHITE LINEN AND HAS BEEN EMBELLISHED WITH WOODEN BUTTONS FOUND IN AN INDIAN MARKET. THE CHENILLE CURTAIN AND STITCHED FELT RUG INTRODUCE MORE LAYERS OF WARMTH TO THE ROOM.

ABOVE RIGHT A NATURAL LINEN SOFA IS THE IDEAL BACKDROP FOR CUSHIONS IN DIFFERENT COLOURS AND TEXTURES. THE RED ONE AT THE FAR LEFT IS MADE OF WOOL FELT; NEXT TO THIS IS PLAIN OTTOMAN CHENILLE; WHILE TO THE RIGHT OF THIS IS CHEQUERBOARD CHENILLE – AN INVITING ARRANGEMENT OF WARM TONES AND MATERIALS. THE NEEDLEPOINT BOAT ON THE BLUE CUSHION ADDS CHARACTER AND INTRODUCES A DECORATIVE MOTIF.

BELOW LEFT CONSIDER WEIGHT AND FINISH WHEN CHOOSING FURNISHING FABRICS. THE HEAVYWEIGHT BRUSHED COTTON USED FOR THIS CURTAIN HAS A SLIGHT SHEEN, WHICH ADDS ANOTHER LAYER OF INTEREST TO THE SCHEME. THE RED AND CREAM COLOURWAYS ARE FROM THE SAME FABRIC RANGE, BUT LOOK CHIC WHEN USED TOGETHER IN THIS WAY. EDGING AND LINING CURTAINS IN A CONTRASTING SHADE GIVES THEM DEFINITION AND CREATES A MORE FORMAL, ELEGANT STYLE.

BELOW RIGHT ADD A WITTY TOUCH TO A MATCHING SET OF DINING CHAIRS BY UPHOLSTERING THEM IN DIFFERENT FABRICS. HERE VARIOUS WEIGHTS OF COTTON CHECKS AND STRIPES HAVE BEEN USED, BUT AS THEY ARE FROM THE SAME COLOUR FAMILY THEY HAVE A UNIFIED LOOK. THE FLORAL UNDERCLOTH ANCHORS THEM TOGETHER. THIS IDEA COULD BE REVERSED BY USING THE SAME PATTERN FOR THE UPHOLSTERY, BUT IN AN ARRAY OF DIFFERENT COLOURS.

Combining Fabrics

Whether you wish to use one fabulous texture or pattern in large amounts, or several fabrics in smaller quantities, it is important to consider each one in relation to the others, just as you would with colours. Every fabric that is chosen adds another layer to the decorative scheme and contributes to the overall style and atmosphere of the room.

Combining fabrics is important because the interplay of surfaces against each other brings frissons of interest and delight to an interior scheme. There are endless possible fabric combinations, and the same basic contrasts can be achieved in subtly different ways. Consider, for example, the contrast of hard and soft textures, and compare the effect of placing a cashmere blanket on a leather chair with that of adding a quilted cushion to a tightly upholstered sofa. Such decisions as these help to define the essential character of a room.

The key principles for combining colours were explained in Colour Codes, pages 31–32. The other main qualities to consider when mixing fabrics – Texture, Pattern and Scale – are highlighted over the next few pages. This section includes a further category – Old and New – to demonstrate the wonderful effects that can be created by combining antique and modern textiles.

RIGHT THE PLAIN LINEN CURTAIN AND COTTON GINGHAM BLIND HAVE BEEN ECHOED HERE IN THE LINEN UNION USED FOR THE SOFA.

BELOW RIGHT AN INSET BORDER OF WHITE LINEN ADDS INTEREST TO THIS OATMEAL LINEN CURTAIN. THE COTTON GINGHAM BORDER DEFINES THE LINES BETWEEN CURTAIN AND MATCHING BLIND.

ABOVE DAMASKS ARE TRADITIONALLY ASSOCIATED WITH GRANDEUR, BUT THIS BAY TREE DESIGN ON A LINEN UNION HAS A RUSTIC FLAVOUR.

RIGHT WHITE CALICO UPHOLSTERY CLOTH AND COOL LINEN ARE GIVEN A VISUAL LIFT HERE BY THE JUXTAPOSITION OF AN ANTIQUE WOOLLEN THROW AND DECORATIVE WOOD BUTTONS.

Texture

Texture in fabrics emphasizes mood within a room. A grand dining room is synonymous with velvet, brocade, paisley and taffeta, whereas a romantic bedroom brings to mind voile, piqué, lightweight cotton and ribbon trims. Texture can be used to create the smart town house look of smooth linen, suede and mohair or the rustic ideal of ticking-stripe curtains and jute tie-backs. Every fabric you choose has textural significance, so be aware of how you can use this to add another layer of interest to a room. This applies not just to foundation fabrics, but also to smaller items – denim cushions embellished with wooden buttons are the perfect addition to a relaxed family room, for example, whereas cashmere ones trimmed with satin look sensational on a leather club chair.

ABOVE LEFT THE PALE AQUAS AND DONKEY BROWNS OF THIS WOOL TARTAN UPHOLSTERED CHAIR ARE COMPLEMENTED BY A LINEN CUSHION TRIMMED WITH SHIRT BUTTONS.
ABOVE RIGHT THE CREAM WAFFLE COTTON LOOSE COVER HARMONIZES WITH THE LINEN CUSHION AND SHEER LINEN CURTAINS EMBROIDERED WITH A TRELLIS DESIGN.
BELOW THIS COTTON PIQUÉ CUSHION WITH AN ORNATE SCALLOPED BORDER WORKS PERFECTLY WITH THE DELICATELY PATTERNED COTTON UPHOLSTERY AND SOFT MOHAIR THROW

BELOW MIX PATTERNS WITH CONFIDENCE. BOLD AND BREEZY
CHECKS AND STRIPES PRINTED ON TAFFETA ADD VIGOUR TO THIS
PLAIN GREEN SOFA.

ABOVE DIFFERENT PATTERNS CAN BE EFFECTIVELY COMBINED
ON ONE ITEM. THE CENTRE CUSHION HERE IS HALF SPLENDID
CONVOLVULUS DESIGN AND HALF SIMPLE GINGHAM.

Pattern
Pattern brings personality to a room. Some patterns convey a certain look: toile de Jouy, for example, gives a room a classic feel, whereas tartan signifies cosiness and florals are reminiscent of country romance. The simplest way to mix patterns together is to choose a decorative pattern first, then coordinate a plain or semi-plain fabric and a check or a stripe in a different scale, all in the same colour palette. You can then use combinations of all these fabrics for the window treatment, upholstered furniture and cushions. Consider using a checked fabric for your sofa, and then overlaying it with cushions in different combinations of patterns, for example stripes and checks or a floral with a small gingham check. A footstool or chair can become a more important feature when upholstered in a boldly patterned fabric. Interesting effects can be created by mixing patterns on the same item. Dining chairs, for example, could be upholstered in a mixture of checks and stripes.

ABOVE MOTIFS HAVE BEEN
CUT FROM THIS DUCK-
INSPIRED FABRIC TO MAKE
APPLIQUÉ SQUARES FOR
CUSHIONS IN VARYING
WEIGHTS OF FABRIC.

LEFT THESE CLEVERLY
COORDINATED COTTON
CUSHIONS, IN A MIXTURE OF
FLORALS, STRIPES AND CHECKS,
HAVE PIPING THAT HAS BEEN
CUT ON THE BIAS – WHICH
MEANS CUT ON THE DIAGONAL
– SO THAT IT TOO MAKES
INTERESTING PATTERNS.

BELOW EVEN THE MOST CLASSIC
OF PATTERNS CAN BE USED
TOGETHER. HERE A GLORIOUS
RED DAMASK SITS HAPPILY
WITH A PRINTED FLORAL LINEN
AND A SMART PAISLEY, WITH
A TIMELESS CREAM SOFA AS
THE BACKDROP.

LEFT THIS INTERESTING CURTAIN HAS BEEN MADE OUT OF TWO
DIFFERENT SCALES OF COTTON CHECKS WITH A PRETTY COTTON
TRIMMING SEWN ACROSS THE JOINS.
BELOW THE BROAD STRIPES OF THIS MATELASSÉ TABLECLOTH
HAVE BEEN COMPLEMENTED BY GINGHAM CHECK LOOSE COVERS
IN A DIFFERING SCALE ON THE CHAIR.

Scale
Using pattern allows you to explore the
significance of scale within a room. A mix of scales
in individual rooms and throughout the home adds
variety and interest. A larger-scale pattern can be
used to create a focal point, with a smaller-scale
design in a supporting role. For example, you
could use a large-scale damask on an armchair
with a small-scale stripe on a cushion. Scale is an
invaluable way of imprinting a style onto a room.
The larger the scale, the more important an
interior can appear to be. Smaller-scale patterns,
such as a coordinating fabric and wallpaper, can
bring charm to an interior and are often the key
element of a pretty scheme. Juxtaposing scales
such as gingham checks in the same colours can
create a very smart look.

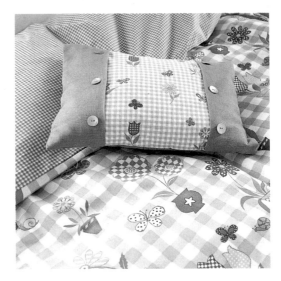

ABOVE RIGHT THE EASIEST WAY TO MIX SCALES IS TO CHOOSE
PATTERNS FROM A COORDINATING RANGE. THIS FUN FLORAL
CAN BE USED LARGE FOR THE BEDSPREAD OR SMALL FOR THE
CUSHION, WHILE PLAIN BLUE COTTON AND PEARL BUTTONS
EMBELLISH THE LOOK.
BOTTOM RIGHT SIMILARLY, IN THIS RANGE, WHICH WAS
INSPIRED BY AMERICAN FOLK ART WEATHER-VANES, THE MAIN
FABRIC IS PERFECT FOR CURTAINS WHILE THE SMALLER VERSION
IS IDEAL FOR THE CHAIR CUSHION.

THIS SMART TABLE RUNNER HAS BEEN MADE
OUT OF TWO CHECKS DESIGNED TO BE USED
TOGETHER AND COLOURED FROM THE SAME
DYE. NOTE HOW THE CHANGE OF SCALE
OCCURS AT THE EDGE OF THE TABLE.

BELOW OLD REMNANTS CAN BE COMBINED TOGETHER ON ONE ITEM. THIS NAUTICALLY INSPIRED CUSHION IS A MIXTURE OF ANTIQUE LINEN AND OLD COTTON STRIPE. THE BOAT MOTIF IS ALSO MADE FROM OLD FABRICS.

Old and new
Incorporating old textiles into a room is a wonderful way of injecting individuality into a scheme. Often they have been woven and printed using methods that are no longer practised today, so they have a character which is impossible to replicate in modern fabrics. It isn't necessary to salvage a full-size pair of curtains to mix old with new. A length of antique textile can be bordered and lined with a new contrasting fabric to create a curtain or blind. Even a scrap of a beautiful antique fabric can be used for a cushion or a piece of patchwork. Think laterally when looking for fabrics: old linen sheets can make glorious tablecloths or curtains, while blankets can be transformed into seat cushions or even upholstered on a chair. It is often the old trimmings that are worth reusing. Pieces of fan edging, braids and tassels that were often hand woven can be applied to cushions or used to trim the edge of a throw. They can also be used as, or applied to, curtain tie-backs. If you find a lovely old fragment that you cannot think of a use for, then consider having it framed.

ABOVE THIS ANTIQUE WING-BACK CHAIR IS UPHOLSTERED IN ITS ORIGINAL TICKING STRIPE FABRIC. THE NEW COTTON CUSHIONS HAVE BEEN GIVEN A TWIST WITH APPLIQUÉD GINGHAM CHECK HEARTS CROSS-STITCHED ONTO THEIR TOPS.

LEFT IF YOU HAVE A PIECE OF OLD FABRIC THAT IS TOO SHORT FOR THE USE YOU HAVE IN MIND, CONSIDER BORDERING THE CENTRAL ANTIQUE PIECE WITH STRIPS OF NEW FABRIC TO MAKE IT GO FURTHER, AS HERE.

RIGHT OLD AND NEW FABRICS IN SIMILAR SHADES WORK WELL TOGETHER. HERE AN ANTIQUE FLORAL IN BROWN AND BEIGE HAS BEEN BORDERED WITH A SIMILARLY OLD TRELLIS DESIGN. HOWEVER, THE BLUE BACKING IS NEW. THE STRIPE IS ALSO OLD BUT HAS BEEN EMBELLISHED WITH A NEW COTTON FRINGE.

BELOW RIGHT PATCHWORK IS ANOTHER GOOD WAY OF USING OLD PIECES OF FABRIC, AS IT DOES NOT REQUIRE FINELY HONED NEEDLEWORK SKILLS. THE CENTRAL PANEL OF THIS DECORATIVE CUSHION IS ANTIQUE, BUT THE PRINTED LINEN BACKGROUND AND OXFORD BORDER ARE NEW.

BOTTOM RIGHT THE CHECK ON THE LEFT IS AN OLD FABRIC WITH NEW PIPING THAT HAS BEEN CUT ON THE BIAS. ON THE RIGHT IS A MODERN EQUIVALENT IN A LARGER SCALE.

BELOW LEFT THE ANTIQUE RED-AND-BEIGE TICKING STRIPE ON THE RIGHT HAS A VERY DIFFERENT CHARACTER TO ITS CONTEMPORARY COMPANIONS, BUT THEY ALL WORK WELL TOGETHER.

Curtains and Blinds

Curtains and blinds provide comfort and privacy, and can have a major impact on the mood of a room. A grand damask hung in a dining room creates a totally different atmosphere to a cotton print in a family room. There are many factors to bear in mind when choosing window treatments, not just colour, texture and pattern, but also the weight and opacity of the materials, and the type of headings and fixings.

The view outside

Before considering the different options for window treatments, it is important to think about their purpose. First, look at the window and the view beyond. If your home is in a private location with a marvellous vista, you may want only the most minimal of window coverings. If, on the other hand, you are open to public gaze and the view outside is not so attractive, you may prefer a solution that preserves your privacy while allowing light into the room.

Decide also whether to dress the windows so they are sympathetic to the view beyond, or whether to choose a more striking treatment that stops the eye. If the environment outside is full of strong colours – like the blue of the sea or the terracotta of a brick wall – allow these shades to influence the materials you choose for curtains or blinds. Windows are, after all, the link between indoors and out.

This can work both ways, of course. If your window looks out onto a busy street, you may wish to make it look attractive from the outside by using a coloured or patterned lining for your curtains. Choosing a lining fabric that unifies all the rooms facing the street, such as a simple check, will have an especially pleasing effect when seen as a whole.

THIS PAGE AND OPPOSITE HUNG FROM A SIMPLE WOODEN POLE, THIS UNUSUAL PATCHWORK CURTAIN HAS BEEN MADE FROM AN EMBROIDERED DESIGN WITH A BASKET MOTIF, A PLAIN BLUE FABRIC, ASSORTED BEIGE CHECKS AND STRIPES AND A HORIZONTAL BAND OF TAUPE. BOTH THIS AND THE STRIPED COTTON BLIND HAVE BEEN EDGED WITH ROPE IN AN ACCENT COLOUR OF NAVY BLUE.

Light and temperature

Window treatments can be used to determine how much natural light comes into a room and how it falls. Blinds, café curtains, voiles and louvred shutters allow light to filter in, while maintaining privacy. Stretching coloured or patterned voile between two poles to form a panel is a lovely way of achieving both aims. If you want to minimize strong sunlight in a room, perhaps to protect furniture or paintings, roller blinds are an effective solution.

In temperate climates consider changing the window treatment to suit the season, with for example a full and heavy curtain to shut out winter cold, but a lighter, more transparent solution in summer.

OPPOSITE THE PLAIN LINEN BLIND AND CURTAIN AT THE WINDOW ON THE LEFT HAVE BEEN SUBTLY EMBELLISHED FOR ADDED INTEREST. THE BLIND IS BORDERED WITH WHITE LINEN, WHILE THE LEADING EDGE OF THE CURTAIN IS TRIMMED WITH GINGHAM CHECK. THIS HAS ALSO BEEN USED AS A LINING FOR THE CURTAIN AND BLIND, UNIFYING THE WINDOW FROM THE OUTSIDE. THE CURTAIN OVER THE ADJACENT GLASS DOOR IS MADE OUT OF A LIGHTWEIGHT LINEN THAT ALLOWS LIGHT TO FILTER INTO THE ROOM. THE VALANCE IS ALSO BORDERED WITH WHITE.

Window proportions

Window treatments can also be masters of disguise. To make a narrow window appear wider, fix a curtain pole to extend beyond the window, then hang the curtains so they cover the wall. Hanging curtains to cover the window and very little of the adjacent wall will make a window appear narrower. Blinds are good for improving window proportions as they impose a sense of geometry on their surroundings.

Curtains and blinds can also help to disguise badly proportioned rooms. To make a room appear taller, hang the curtains from ceiling to floor, rather than from the top of the window. To lower a ceiling visually, use pelmets, which will draw the eye to a lower level.

Linking rooms

Consider each window in relation to others in the house, and how colour, texture, pattern and scale flow from one space to the next. For example, a living room with neutral curtains and patterned upholstery can be linked to an adjoining room with the same pattern at the windows and a coordinating stripe on the chairs.

Windows can be dressed to act as focal points. If you have a vista within the house, such as a view from the front door through the hall to a window in a room beyond, a beautiful window treatment will draw people into the house.

BELOW THESE UNLINED LINEN CURTAINS HAVE BEEN GIVEN A DECORATIVE HEADING OF A GINGHAM CHECK VALANCE BORDERED WITH NAVY BLUE TRIM, WHICH IS ECHOED IN THE RUNNER ON THE TABLE.

ABOVE TIE-BACKS CAN BE USED TO CONTINUE A THEME WITHIN A ROOM. THESE ONES ARE MADE FROM ROPE AND BOAT CLEATS AND ARE PERFECT FOR A NAUTICAL THEME. THE CURTAIN IS A LIGHTWEIGHT WINDOW-PANE CHECK LINED WITH A SEA-BLUE COTTON.

Window treatment style

Decide whether the window treatment is to be a central feature of the scheme or whether it should have less prominence. If you want it to stand out, choose strong colours and bold patterns or a decorative heading and dramatic trimmings. Otherwise opt for plains and neutrals and add interest through texture. Striped curtains and blinds always look smart – choose narrow stripes for a relaxed mood and broader ones for a grander effect.

Also take into account the architecture of the room. Tie-backs, for instance, will rarely suit a room with very graphic lines, as they bunch the curtain fabric up rather than allowing it to fall in folds. A period home will suit more traditional types of curtain treatments, for example goblet headings or decorative pelmets. In modern homes simple curtain treatments or Roman blinds are usually more appropriate.

Choose colours and patterns carefully. Ask for the biggest sample available and pin it to the window for a week or so to ensure you make the right choice. If the fabric is patterned, it should be the first fabric you choose for the scheme: it is generally much easier to match plains to patterns than vice versa.

Practical considerations

Bear in mind the use of the room when deciding on window treatments. Steamy bathrooms, for example, need a practical material such as wooden shutters or pinoleum blinds. In kitchens choose fabrics that are easy to clean, preferably washable.

Curtain headings should also be appropriate to the location. For example, ribbon ties with pretty voiles are more for show than for use, and are best avoided in children's rooms if they are likely to be subjected to heavy pulls.

The success of a window treatment depends not just on the fabric, but on the quality of the making. It is important to be generous with fabric: better to have beautifully made calico curtains that are double width and hang well, than silk ones that have been skimped on.

The placement of the pattern is critical. Curtains with a strong motif, such as a flower, must be made in such a way that it is not cut off at the top. Similarly, the pattern on a blind should look attractive when it is both folded and unfolded. A good curtain or blind maker will calculate how much fabric is needed to achieve the correct pattern placement.

1
CONTRASTING
FABRIC TIES.
2
DECORATIVE
FINIAL WITH
SIMPLE PINCH
PLEATS.
3
CAFE CLIPS
ON RINGS.
4
INFORMAL
PULLED AND
GATHERED
HEADING.

5
SELF-
FRINGING ON
A VALANCE.
6
DECORATIVE
PINCH PLEATS
WITH
CONTRAST
EDGING.
7
ALTERNATING
COLOURED
TIES.
8
CONTRASTING
FABRIC
BUTTONS ON
PINCH
PLEATS.

9
SMALL
GOBLET
HEADING.
10
UNGATHERED
HEADING
TIED ON A
POLE.
11
STEEL POLE
WITH
EYELETS.
12
THIN WIRE
POLE AND
CLIPS.

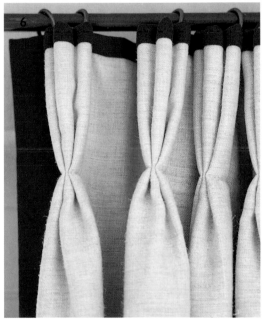

There is no 'correct' length for curtains; it is a matter of personal choice. However, bear in mind that if you want to use tie-backs, the length of the curtains will shorten. Lined curtains always look elegant, but unlined ones can also be wonderful, particularly in a heavy fabric such as a printed velvet.

Lateral thinking

There is plenty of scope for creating individual window treatments. One option is to buy a simple curtain or blind and make it unique. Ready-made curtains can be customized with buttons, borders, ribbons, trims or appliqué.

Existing curtains can often be given a fresh look by exchanging pelmets for poles, or by adding a new border or trim. Antique braids and trims are also a lovely way of changing the look of a pair of curtains.

Be adventurous when choosing materials for curtains: use anything from green billiard cloth for the winter, to check cotton napkins stitched together for the summer. You may find an unusual fabric on holiday, or fragments that can be used to make patchwork curtains. Unusual fabric combinations also work well – a coarse linen edged with jewel-coloured velvet, for example, or wool bordered with satin. Adding a patterned trim to a simple pair of curtains gives them a more stylish look.

Tie-backs need not be made of fabric: twine, ribbon, velvet, jute and leather all make unusual alternatives. Enliven poles and pelmets by covering them with fabric, painting them in coordinating shades or painting curtain rings in contrasting colours.

There are many ways of customizing blinds. They can, for example, be appliquéd with other fabrics, bordered with rope, or stencilled.

If in doubt . . .

If you are unsure what to do but cannot live with bare windows or the existing curtains any longer, buy simple white or cream blinds to hook over the windows while you get to know the space better.

A longer-term solution that's guaranteed to work is to buy a lovely pair of cream curtains. There are many timeless fabrics to choose from, including linen, damask, velvet, calico, weaves and silk. To finish a curtain, apply a 3 centimetre binding of contrasting or coloured fabric down the leading edge; this could be coordinated with another highlight colour in the room. The smartest and simplest curtain treatment is to use poles with pinch-pleat-headed curtains.

1 BLIND WITH FITTED PELMET.
2 VERTICAL STRIPE USED HORIZONTALLY ON BLIND.
3 SAIL CURTAIN ON HOOKS.
4 ROMAN BLIND TRIMMED WITH ACCENT OF GREEN.
5 ROLLED-UP SHEER BLIND CONTRAST BOUND WITH ACCENT COLOUR.
6 ROMAN BLINDS OF TOILE WITH CRIMSON EDGING.
7 BOLD CHECKED ROMAN BLIND.
8 APPLIQUÉD ELEPHANT MOTIF ON PLAIN BLIND.
9 BLIND WITH FLORAL DESIGN SHOWING CORRECT PLACEMENT OF PATTERN AT TOP.
10 DETAIL OF BLIND SHOWN IN 9 ILLUSTRATING GREEN GINGHAM EDGING
11 PAINTED WOODEN SHUTTERS.

Upholstery

Upholstery fabrics are critical to the success of an interior. As well as covering and protecting furniture, they also endow a scheme with visual and tactile comfort. In design terms, they contribute much to the style and atmosphere of a room, and create a sense of harmony and balance by linking furniture with the walls, floor and window treatment.

Good planning is vital to choosing upholstery. List all the upholstered pieces you want to include in the room and sketch them onto a floor plan (see pages 14–15). A list for a living room, for example, may include a sofa, armchairs, occasional chairs, stools or ottomans, and window seats. Consider how each item relates to the others and how it fits into the scheme. Also decide whether you want to change the layout of the furniture for different seasons or when entertaining, and ensure that your fabric choices will work in these different configurations.

Furniture shape

Fabrics should always be chosen to complement the shape and style of the furniture to be upholstered. A classic item such as a scroll-arm sofa would suit any fabric from a plain weave to a damask or a decorative print. A modern armchair with more graphic lines will suit a plain, textured fabric. Antique chairs or sofas may benefit from a more decorative upholstery treatment, such as silk or velvet, a stripe or a tapestry fabric. Using different colours, patterns and scales can make an item of furniture appear wider, narrower, lower or higher, depending on the effect you want to create. If the furniture has attractive legs, choose an upholstery finish that will complement this feature.

Assess how the item to be upholstered will look in the room from all angles. For example, will a sofa be seen from the front, the back, or both directions? If the piece is to be placed in an alcove, this is an opportunity to make your budget go further by using a more expensive fabric on the front and a cheaper one on the back. It is also important to decide at this stage if you want to have loose covers made for any of the items as these too will play a part in the decorative scheme.

Upholstery style

Given the huge choice of fabrics available, it is important to have a clear idea of what you require. First decide on the overall look you want to create, whether it's classic and tailored, relaxed and informal, cool and crisp or warm and soft. Seek inspiration in books, magazines and furniture catalogues, and by visiting furniture stores. When considering styles, remember the importance of comfort and the key role played by texture in this respect.

Once you have chosen a style, think about the use and distribution of plain and patterned fabrics around the room. As a rule it is easier to choose plain or neutral fabrics for major items such as sofas as these have a timeless appeal. More colourful or luxurious textiles can be used on smaller items to provide focal points. Fabrics on larger items should also bring a textural dimension to the scheme. Heavy linens, herringbone designs and small textured weaves are ideal.

The other advantage of choosing plain fabrics for large pieces is that they make it easier to change the style and mood of a room. Colour and pattern can be introduced onto sofas and chairs through cushions, throws and runners, and the transition from winter to summer is simple to achieve (see Timely Changes, pages 162–165).

LEFT ABOVE
THE BLUE PAINTED LEGS OF THIS OLD CHAIR MAKE THE PERFECT FOIL FOR THE BLUE TICKING STRIPE UPHOLSTERY. THE THROW ADDS WARMTH IN WINTER.

LEFT BELOW
KICK-PLEAT CORNERS ARE A SMART-LOOKING SOLUTION FOR SOFAS AND CHAIRS WITHOUT LEGS.

OPPOSITE
PLAIN LINEN IS THE FOUNDATION FABRIC IN THIS COMFORTABLE LIVING ROOM, AND HAS BEEN USED BOTH FOR THE SOFA AND THE FOOTSTOOL. THE LATTER CAN BE COVERED WITH A BLANKET THROW IN WINTER.

Solutions for smaller pieces range from decorative designs, such as florals, to more tailored patterns, such as stripes. The fabric could be a design from a current collection, an antique remnant you have salvaged, or a treasure brought back from abroad. Introducing a small piece of unusual or luxurious fabric can lift the entire scheme. It is always easier to match a plain fabric to a patterned one, so make the latter your starting point, even though it may be being used in relatively small quantities.

Small chairs, such as fireside chairs, offer lots of scope for experimenting with fabrics because they do not dominate a scheme. You could, for example, choose a check in two scales, and use one for the seat and one for the back; or use a pattern for the seat and a plain for the back. If you have a matching pair of chairs, consider reversing the combination. Such chairs are also ideal for hand-sewn pieces, for example embroidery or tapestry, or glamorous fabrics like suede or silk.

If you are cautious about using colour or pattern, upholster everything within the room in two colours. These might be two neutrals, such as biscuit and cream, or two sympathetic plains, such as dark blue and taupe. You can then use smaller items, such as cushions, rugs and lampshades, to introduce vitality. If you have small occasional chairs, consider introducing a third colour. One of the three colours could relate to the curtains or blinds.

It is possible to build up an elaborately decorated look by introducing many more patterns and colours into the room through throws and cushions. This will be easier if you choose several plain colours in luxurious weaves for the foundation fabrics and add decorative patterns for the curtains and smaller items of upholstery.

If you are overwhelmed by the vast range of upholstery fabrics and trimmings it is wise to seek the advice of a professional decorator or upholsterer.

Practical considerations

Choose fabrics that will be practical for the way the room is used. Most upholstery fabrics today show a rub test for durability: 12,000 to 15,000 rubs is acceptable for areas of normal domestic use; 10,000 rubs is recommended only for light use. Consider also how easy fabrics are to clean, or have loose covers made that can be washed or dry cleaned. Loose covers need not be left plain but can be embellished with appliqué work, buttons, ribbon, trims or contrast piping.

FAR LEFT
BULLION FRINGING
INTRODUCES A FORMAL
NOTE TO A SCHEME. THIS
EXAMPLE HAS BEEN
MADE IN CREAM COTTON
TO COMPLEMENT THE
PLAIN UPHOLSTERY.
CENTRE LEFT
LOOSE COVERS ON SOFAS
ADD INFORMALITY AND,
BEING WASHABLE, ARE
VERY PRACTICAL IN
FAMILY ROOMS.
NEAR LEFT
CONTRAST PIPING CAN
MAKE A PLAIN PIECE OF
FURNITURE LOOK VERY
SMART – CREAM AGAINST
BLUE IS A CLASSIC
CHOICE.

FAR LEFT
THE SCROLL ARMS OF
THIS SOFA HAVE BEEN
SELF PIPED, BUT THE
FABRIC IS BIAS CUT FOR
A DECORATIVE LOOK.
CENTRE LEFT
CONTRASTING FABRICS
HAVE BEEN USED FOR
THE BODY OF THIS SOFA
AND THE SEAT CUSHIONS.
THE CUSHION FABRIC IS
ALSO USED FOR THE
CONTRAST PIPING ON
THE ARMS.
NEAR LEFT
THIS VIEW OF THE SOFA
SEEN LEFT SHOWS HOW
VITAL IT IS TO POSITION
BOLD MOTIFS CENTRALLY
ON KEY ITEMS.

FAR LEFT
SIMPLE BEIGE-AND-
CREAM COTTON CHECKS
ON PLUMP SEATING
CREATE AN ATMOSPHERE
OF WELCOME.
CENTRE LEFT
PATTERN CAN BE
INTRODUCED VERY
SUBTLY, AS WITH THIS
QUIET BROAD STRIPE ON
A LINEN UNION FABRIC.
NEAR LEFT
CONSIDER THE
PLACEMENT OF PATTERN
CAREFULLY WHEN USING
A DECORATIVE FABRIC.
HERE ROSE MOTIFS ON
TRELLISWORK ARE
ALIGNED ALONG THE
BOTTOM OF THE SOFA.

As with curtains and blinds, if you are using patterned fabrics, think about the placement of the pattern – for example, large motifs should be centred on seat covers or chair backs.

Upholstery trims

Choose upholstery trims to suit the style of the furniture and the room. Very simple interiors call for unobtrusive trims, while pretty and more decorative spaces require a more elaborate finish. Bullion fringing conveys a mood of grandeur and is usually found in more formal living rooms.

The easiest way to make a feature of a sofa or chair is to use a contrasting colour or pattern for the edging rather than a matching one. This gives the same level of finish as binding a curtain edge. A patterned sofa looks wonderful when

RIGHT
FURNITURE THAT IS
USUALLY FOUND IN A
CONSERVATORY CAN BE
GIVEN A SOPHISTICATED
TWIST WITH LOOSE
COVERS OVER CUSHIONS.
THE FORMAL STRIPES ON
THE SEAT AND BACK
MAKE THIS WICKER
CHAIR THE HEIGHT OF
ELEGANCE.

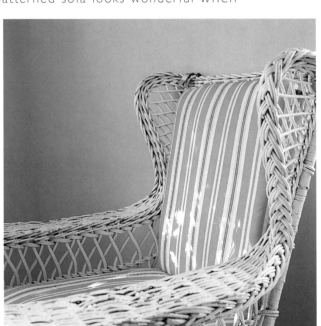

contrast bound in a plain colour, just as a plain sofa does when bound in a contrasting colour or pattern. As well as producing a more elegant effect, it is an excellent way of emphasizing a highlight colour used elsewhere in the scheme.

Applying a gathered skirt to a chair can work well in a pretty bedroom, while a tailored skirt with box pleats looks smart on a dining chair. The skirt can either match or coordinate with the main upholstery fabric on the chair. For example a cream-and-taupe check fabric could be used for the main upholstery and plain taupe for the skirt.

If you have button-backed furniture, choose a plain fabric or one with an all-over pattern so that it does not matter where the upholstery design meets the buttons. You can either make the buttons blend into the background by covering

FAR LEFT
HERE AN ANTIQUE
REMNANT HAS BEEN
MADE INTO A TOP COVER
FOR A SEAT CUSHION.
CENTRE LEFT
THESE LOOSE COVERS
HAVE BEEN CREATED
FROM HUGE PIECES OF
COTTON CALICO,
WRAPPED AROUND THE
CHAIRS AND HELD
TOGETHER WITH
DECORATIVE TIES.
NEAR LEFT
THE TIES SEEN LEFT ARE
STRIPS OF MATCHING
CALICO ADORNED WITH
VIBRANT RED BRAID.

FAR LEFT
WHEN UPHOLSTERING
A BUTTON-BACK PIECE,
CHOOSE MATCHING
BUTTONS, AS HERE, OR
CONTRASTING ONES.
CENTRE LEFT
THE PLACEMENT OF A
UNIFORM PATTERN SUCH
AS A STRIPE IS VITAL ON
SYMMETRICAL DESIGNS
LIKE THIS ONE.
NEAR LEFT
A COST-EFFECTIVE WAY
OF UPHOLSTERING A
CHAIR IS TO CHOOSE A
LUXURIOUS FABRIC FOR
THE SEAT, SUCH AS THIS
EMBROIDERED CHENILLE,
AND A LESS EXPENSIVE
CLOTH FOR THE BACK.

FAR LEFT
TO MAKE IT COSIER,
THIS MODERN CHAIR
HAS BEEN TIGHTLY
UPHOLSTERED IN RICH
RED CHENILLE WITH
SELF PIPING.
CENTRE LEFT
EVEN A LOOSE COVER
NEEDS PLANNING TO
ENSURE THE PATTERN IS
PLACED CORRECTLY.
NEAR LEFT
ONE OF THE LEAST
EXPENSIVE WAYS OF
UPHOLSTERING A CHAIR
IS TO COVER IT WITH
COTTON CALICO, THE
IDEAL BACKDROP FOR
THROWS AND CUSHIONS.

them with the same fabric or make them more prominent by using a contrasting pattern, such as checked buttons against a plain fabric or blue buttons against a cream one.

Dining chairs

Dining chairs offer great scope for creativity with fabrics. A set of matching chairs always looks smart but you can inject more vitality into a dining room by using contrasting colours or patterns. There are two simple options: use the same fabric in two different colours or use the same colour in two different patterns. You could, for example, choose a blue floral design for the seat cushion and a blue stripe or check for the back. You could even alternate the chairs around the table from stripes to checks. Once you begin experimenting in this

way, you will realize how many possibilities there are. You may have an arrangement, for example, where half the chairs are red and half are green; or where half are red with green backs and half are green with red backs.

Matching buttons or ribbon-ties down the back of each chair add a further decorative detail – remember that a dining chair is one item of furniture that is often viewed from the back.

Drop-in seats provide an easy means of ringing the seasonal changes. Rich velvets are ideal for winter use, while simple ginghams are perfect for summer. As with loose covers, the seats need not match. Each one can be a different colour or you could choose two shades and alternate them around the table. Use contrast binding to give them even greater definition.

OPPOSITE TOP THIS SMART, FORMAL DINING ROOM HAS BEEN GIVEN A PRETTY LOOK BY COVERING BALLOON-BACKED CHAIRS WITH LOOSE COVERS IN BEIGE GINGHAM, HELD BY MATCHING TIES. THE CLOTH ON THE TABLE IS A SUMPTUOUS MATELASSÉ FABRIC, WHICH ANCHORS THE OTHER COLOURS.

OPPOSITE CENTRE LEFT IN THIS COOL, ELEGANT DINING ROOM WICKER CHAIRS HAVE BEEN LOOSE-COVERED IN PLAIN LINEN HELD IN PLACE WITH NAVY-BLUE TIES. THIS IS IN HARMONY WITH THE OTHER COLOURS IN THE ROOM. THE CLOTH ON THE TABLE IS AN ANTIQUE LINEN FABRIC.

OPPOSITE CENTRE RIGHT THE CHAIR PICTURED ABOVE HAS HERE BEEN LOOSE-COVERED IN PLAIN LINEN, WHICH GIVES IT A DIFFERENT CHARACTER TO THE INFORMAL GINGHAM. BY SHROUDING THE SHAPE OF THE CHAIR, ATTENTION IS FOCUSED ON THE ELEGANTLY TAPERED LEGS.

OPPOSITE BOTTOM HERE THE CHAIRS SEEN LEFT HAVE BEEN FINISHED WITH A BLUE SEERSUCKER TRIM THAT IS PIPED AROUND THE BOTTOM TO MATCH THE TIES. THIS GIVES DEFINITION TO THE SHAPE OF THE CHAIR AND BECOMES AN ACCENT COLOUR WITHIN THE SCHEME.

TOP BECAUSE DINING CHAIRS NEED RELATIVELY LITTLE FABRIC COMPARED WITH SOFAS AND ARMCHAIRS, IT MAY BE WORTH CONSIDERING A SLIGHTLY MORE EXPENSIVE OPTION. THIS EMBROIDERED FABRIC HAS A TEXTURAL QUALITY THAT ADDS TO ITS BEAUTY. A TINY FRINGE HAS BEEN USED TO EDGE THE TIGHTLY COVERED SEATS.

CENTRE LEFT ONE OF THE SIMPLEST WAYS TO GIVE DINING CHAIRS A DECORATIVE TOUCH IS TO ADD TIE-ON PIECES OF FABRIC, SUCH AS THE FLORAL DESIGN SEEN HERE. RING THE CHANGES BY USING DIFFERENT FABRICS TO SUIT THE SEASON OR THE OCCASION.

CENTRE RIGHT THE TICKING STRIPE USED ON THESE SEAT BACKS PROVIDES AN INTERESTING CONTRAST WITH THE PRETTY PEAR TREE DESIGN. BEING CHEAPER, IT IS ALSO A COST-EFFECTIVE SOLUTION IF YOU NEED TO UPHOLSTER SEVERAL DINING CHAIRS.

BOTTOM LOOSE COVERS NEED NOT BE INFORMAL: THE CHAIRS SEEN HERE HAVE QUITE THE OPPOSITE LOOK WHEN COVERED WITH A BOLD EMBROIDERED CHECK BOUND WITH RED PIPING AT THE BOTTOM FOR EMPHASIS. KICK-PLEAT CORNERS ACCENTUATE THE FORMALITY.

Cushions

Cushions add comfort, character and colour to a room. They are also one of the simplest ways of giving a scheme a visual lift, whether it is in a living room, a bedroom or a children's room. A plain-coloured sofa or armchair makes the perfect base on which to introduce tone, pattern and texture through cushions, while with a decorative upholstery fabric they provide a way of drawing out the richness of the design. Cushions can be chosen either to coordinate with other elements of the scheme, such as curtains, rugs or wall coverings, or to inject a new layer of interest.

Cushion style

Almost any fabric is suitable for making cushions, including a mixture of old and new textiles. You can sew them, knit them or even stencil designs onto silk. Use whatever is appropriate to your scheme – paisley, tartan, chenille, lace, patchwork, crewelwork, velvet, silk, wool or a printed fabric.

Textures can be mixed by combining different weights of fabric: suede with linen, for example, or cotton with silk. In the summer, consider making loose covers from voile and putting these over plain-coloured fabrics.

Cushions can be embellished in the same way as curtains or upholstery. Trims, feathers, ribbons, fringes and bobbles will create a decorative look, while old horn, wood or pearl buttons offer a more subtle form of ornamentation.

Uses of cushions

As well as choosing cushions for their visual qualities, consider their practical usefulness. A square shape measuring at least 55 x 55 centimetres will be generous enough to offer good back support, while cushions placed on chairs and window seats must be deep and wide enough to provide comfort. Floor cushions bring a relaxed, friendly atmosphere to a room. They are popular with children and provide a comfortable place to read or play board games.

Small needlepoint or painted cushions have little practical purpose, but they are a lovely way of introducing a decorative theme or a motif such as dogs, roses or boats. Shapes, too, can vary, so mix squares with rectangles, bolsters, round and even heart or star shapes.

ABOVE CUSHIONS OFFER UNLIMITED SCOPE FOR COMBINING DIFFERENT WEIGHTS, SCALES, TEXTURES, COLOURS AND PATTERNS OF FABRIC. THIS SIMPLE BLUE GINGHAM CUSHION HAS BEEN EDGED WITH AN OXFORD BORDER IN PLAIN CREAM-COLOURED LINEN, WHICH FRAMES IT AND GIVES IT MORE DEFINITION IN THE ROOM.

1 THESE SPRIGGED, TOILE AND STRIPED CUSHIONS ARE ENHANCED BY BRAIDING AND RUFFLES.
2 THIS NAUTICAL NEEDLEPOINT DESIGN INTRODUCES BOTH TEXTURE AND A DECORATIVE LAYER.
3 PAISLEY STRIPES EMBELLISH THE SIDE OF THIS VELVET SEAT CUSHION.
4 AN ANTIQUE CUSHION EMBELLISHED WITH A MONOGRAM.

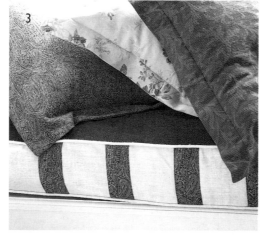

5 CUSHIONS MADE FROM A COMBINATION OF FABRICS, WITH TRIMS AND BUTTONS.
6 A PATCHWORK CUSHION MADE OF PLAIN BLUE COTTON AND A COORDINATING TICKING STRIPE.
7 GINGHAM HEARTS CROSS-STITCHED ONTO COTTON FOR A FOLK-ART EFFECT.
8 STRONG DECORATIVE PATTERNS SUCH AS THESE NEED NOTHING TO EMBELLISH THEM.
9 THE PUCKERED RIBBON ON THIS CUSHION CREATES A CHEQUERBOARD EFFECT, PUNCTUATED BY BUTTONS.

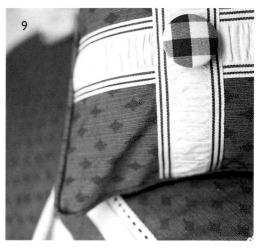

Table dressing

A beautifully dressed table will enhance any meal. Tablecloths, napkins, runners and accessories can help to transform a room from summer to winter, from day to evening, from an informal family lunch to a formal celebration dinner.

Table linen

One of the first things to consider is the surface of the table. If it is beautifully polished or textured wood or has a painted design, it is worth showing off, so do without a tablecloth and use place mats. Hard mats are more practical for protecting wood from hot plates. However, soft mats offer a fair amount of heat-resistance and you can have them made to your own design, which could then be echoed in the napkins.

Another option that allows the table surface to be seen is to use place mats for dining and a runner at other times. These could be coordinated with table linen and loose covers used on the dining chairs.

If you would rather use a tablecloth, decide whether it should provide a calm canvas for your tableware or form a more decorative backdrop. There is a wide range of fabrics available, from crisp white linens for dinner parties to informal gingham checks for brunch. If you want flexibility, a rough-textured linen cloth in cream or taupe is a sensible option.

A combination of cloths of different sizes, placed one over the other, can work well too. Choose fabrics in contrasting colours or textures, such as smooth linen over velvet. You could also vary the shapes. On a round table, for example, place a square cloth over a circular one.

You need not be confined to a conventional tablecloth. Alternatives include antique curtains, sari fabrics, even a fine check wool blanket – remember though that fabrics intended for everyday use should be durable and easy to clean. Embellishments for tablecloths include ribbon trims, velvet borders or runners that lie across the surface.

If you are having loose covers made for dining chairs, consider coordinating them with the tablecloth. One option is to cover the chairs with two coordinating fabrics – a floral and a gingham check, for example – and have two tablecloths made in these fabrics. The tablecloths could then be used to create different looks.

TOP WHEN DRESSING THE TABLE FOR AN AL FRESCO LUNCH, THINK ABOUT HOW YOU CAN MAKE A LINK FROM THE OUTSIDE TO THE INSIDE AND FROM THE TABLE TO THE SURROUNDINGS. HERE THE GREEN GINGHAM UNDERCLOTH PICKS OUT THE COLOURS OF THE COURTYARD. THE DECORATIVE RUNNER OVER THE TOP IS EMBROIDERED WITH GREEN BAY TREES IN BLUE POTS, ECHOING THE BLUE IN THE HOUSE. THIS MOTIF IS REFLECTED IN THE BLUE VASES FILLED WITH GREENERY.

BOTTOM AND OPPOSITE INSIDE THE HOUSE, BLUE RUNNERS WITH COORDINATING SEAT CUSHIONS MAKE AN EYE-CATCHING COMBINATION. THE CHECK OF THE RUNNERS HAS BEEN REPEATED IN THE CURTAIN VALANCE, WHILE THE DECORATIVE BORDER HAS BEEN USED FOR THE CUSHION IN THE FOREGROUND. THE USE OF ONE COLOUR WITH CREAM OR WHITE IS VERY POWERFUL.

LEFT A FULLY COORDINATED LOOK HAS BEEN ACHIEVED IN THIS RELAXED DINING ROOM. THE CHAIRS ARE UPHOLSTERED IN A PEAR TREE DESIGN WITH A TICKING STRIPE ON THE BACK. THIS HAS BEEN REPEATED IN THE RUNNER, MADE FROM THE PEAR TREE FABRIC WITH A BLUE CHECK BORDER. BLUE GLASSES BRING OUT ONE OF THE KEY COLOURS IN THE SCHEME. EVEN THE RUG IS A SCALED-UP VERSION OF THE CHECK.

BELOW LEFT THE RUNNER, TRIMMED WITH A BOBBLE FRINGE, GIVES THE TABLE A LOOK THAT IS BOTH FORMAL AND PRETTY. IT PREVENTS THE DINING ROOM LOOKING TOO STERILE WHEN NOT IN USE AND IS AN IDEAL WAY OF MAKING A LINK BETWEEN TEXTILES AND TABLE.

Finally, when planning how to dress the table for a special occasion, think about the time of day you will be eating, the season, the occasion, the guests and the menu. You could even design the scheme to complement the type of cuisine.

Tableware

People often have a set of everyday china and a formal dinner service. However, if you are short of space or you generally take a relaxed approach to dining, it may make more sense to have mixed china that can be added to as required. Using different tableware for each course can add variety and interest to a meal. For example, a set of decorative dessert plates provides a stylish finish to a special occasion.

Mixing pattern on china follows the same rules as mixing pattern elsewhere in the room. You can combine a plain, a stripe and a decorative design — as long as the colours coordinate. It is also acceptable to mix old plates with new. If you use plates that combine two colours, such as blue and

RIGHT WHEN THE ROOM IS USED FOR INFORMAL DINING, SUCH AS BREAKFASTS AND LUNCHES, THE RUNNER IS REPLACED BY COORDINATING PLACE MATS. IN THE EVENING, A WHITE LINEN OR COTTON TABLECLOTH IS USED TO CHANGE THE MOOD AGAIN, PROVIDING A BACKDROP FOR MORE ELABORATE TABLE SETTINGS. HERE SUNNY YELLOW PLATES HAVE BEEN USED WITH THE BLUE GLASSES, ECHOING ANOTHER COLOUR IN THE PEAR TREE FABRIC.

BELOW RIGHT THE DESIGN OF THE PLACE MATS REVERSES THAT OF THE RUNNER, AS THE CHECK IS USED CENTRALLY WITH A PEAR TREE BORDER. NAPKINS HAVE ALSO BEEN CAREFULLY CHOSEN TO HARMONIZE WITH THE REST OF THE SCHEME.

yellow, you can decide whether to dress the table in blues or yellows, depending on the mood you want to create.

Serving plates and dishes can be used to add an individual touch. Old cheese platters, decorative butter dishes, richly grained wooden salad bowls and wicker bread baskets will all lend character to a table.

Accessories

Coloured glasses make an ordinary table look pretty for relatively little cost. Look for decorative candle holders, a magnificent fruit bowl or a set of silver dessert spoons.

If you include a centrepiece, such as a magnificent bowl of flowers or fruit, make sure people will be able to see each other across the table. Choose an attractive container such as a patterned cachepot or a wire basket. If time is short, think of simple, colourful ideas such as a large bowl of strawberries or a glass vase filled with tulips. For evening meals use candles to add atmosphere and to reflect light off surfaces such as crystal, silver and polished wood.

Bedding

One of the most evocative memories of childhood is of being in bed, tucked under sheets and blankets with hot water bottles and favourite toys. When we choose bedding as an adult, deep down we want to recreate that feeling of being somewhere safe, warm and comfortable. A bedroom should be a personal haven, a sanctuary from the outside world, and the bedding fabrics play a vital part in enhancing this atmosphere.

Bedding style

Bedding should be chosen to suit the look of the bedroom, be it romantic or smart, country or simple. Pattern, scale and colour are important here, so choose bedding with care. Colours can either harmonize or contrast with the scheme and patterns can be mixed, for example by using checked pillowcases with plain ones or florals with stripes.

The tactile qualities of bedding are all-important. Whether you opt for linen or cotton sheets, blankets or duvets, eiderdowns or throws, rectangular pillows or square ones, what matters is how comfortable you feel when you are in bed. Use these interchangeable items to complement other textures in the room through the seasons. For example, use rich blankets in the winter and cotton throws in summer.

Another factor to consider is time. Blankets and sheets give character to a bedroom in a way that duvets do not, but unless you have enough time to make the bed properly every day they are not worth considering. One solution is to use a top sheet with a duvet, so you can fold it over the top as if the duvet were an eiderdown.

White bed linen has an enduring appeal because it always looks fresh and clean. Being timeless, it is a good investment, too. Linen is the first choice for luxury, but it needs a high level of maintenance if you are going to press it properly each time it is washed. Pure cotton sheets are also excellent, with a wonderful crispness when you climb into them.

TOP WHEN DRESSING A BED, FIND ONE KEY PIECE AROUND WHICH ALL THE OTHER BEDDING CAN BE CHOSEN. HERE THE BEDSPREAD IS THE FOUNDATION FOR A COOL, CRISP SCHEME BASED ON BLUE, CREAM AND WHITE.

BOTTOM UNLESS THE BED HAS DECORATIVE LEGS OR YOU ARE USING A VALANCE, CHOOSE A BEDSPREAD THAT IS LARGE ENOUGH TO CONCEAL WHAT LIES BENEATH.

CONSIDER EVERY LAYER WHEN
MAKING A BED BEAUTIFUL.
HERE A LUXURIOUS EGYPTIAN
COTTON SHEET WITH BLUE
REEDED CORD HAS BEEN
COMBINED WITH OXFORD
PILLOWCASES IN BLUE AND
WHITE. THE BEDSPREAD HAS
A RAISED COTTON CHECK
ON THE REVERSE WITH A
MORE FORMAL DECORATIVE
FLORAL ON THE TOP.

Dressing the bed

The look of a bedroom can be changed to suit the seasons by having loose covers made for the headboard. In winter you might use cosy wool or felt, then in summer switch to a pretty voile or a striped cotton. Loose covers are also easier to keep clean than tight upholstery. Use different coloured ribbon ties to complement other colours in the room.

A valance around a bed looks smart if it is coordinated with the headboard. If the headboard and valance are permanent features – rather than being changed seasonally – keep them fairly plain so that you can alter the linen while maintaining the look of the bed. Ticking stripes and checks are good choices if you want to use a pattern. You could bind them in coordinating shades.

Ways of personalizing bed linen include stitching children's names onto the corners of pillowcases or using antique fabrics to appliqué designs onto blankets. Sheets bordered with coloured trims are elegant, while lace sewn onto pillowcases is pretty. Before applying additional textiles to bedlinen ensure they will be colourfast when washed or dry cleaned.

Decorative cushions, such as patchwork or appliqué, can give a bed a finished look. These too can be used to pick out patterns or colours found elsewhere in the room. Add fringing, piping or braiding to finish them off.

Four-poster beds

Whether antique or modern, a four-poster bed hung with a curtain has a wonderful feeling of being cut off from the world outside. Use decorative patterns, sumptuous silks or, the most cost-effective option, romantic voiles. Generous amounts of fabric are needed to create a feeling of luxury and comfort. If using a patterned textile, consider the placement of the pattern from every angle. As a four-poster creates a significant height line in a room, it is important to consider the overall window treatment in relation to the bed, to ensure they harmonize. Children also love four-poster beds, and simple wooden ones are not expensive. Alternatively, a bunk bed can be fitted with a curtain, behind which children will play for hours. Use a decorative voile that allows light through or a practical cotton that can be cleaned easily.

BELOW STEP INTO THE PAST BY MAKING AN OLD-FASHIONED QUILTED EIDERDOWN FROM A MIX OF OLD AND NEW FABRICS. UNLIKE BEDSPREADS, THESE ARE DESIGNED TO SIT ON TOP OF THE BED RATHER THAN COVER THE SIDES TOO. HERE AN ORIGINAL EIDERDOWN HAS BEEN SALVAGED AND GIVEN A NEW COVER, MADE FROM A CONTEMPORARY PRINTED COTTON AND BORDERED WITH AN ANTIQUE REMNANT. THE DECORATIVE TRIM BETWEEN THE FABRICS ALSO HAS A NOSTALGIC LOOK.

OPPOSITE BOTTOM THE EIDERDOWN PICTURED ABOVE IS SHOWN HERE WITH DECORATIVE CUSHIONS THAT ARE ALSO MADE FROM OLD AND NEW FABRICS. THE BOLD BLUE CHECK IS CONTEMPORARY, WHILE THE BLUE AND BEIGE FLORALS AND STRIPES ARE ANTIQUE REMNANTS.

TOP A REMOVABLE RUNNER HAS BEEN MADE FOR THIS HEADBOARD SO THAT IT CAN BE CHANGED OR WASHED EASILY. GREEN GINGHAM IS A PRETTY COMPANION TO THE ROMANTIC TULIP FABRIC AND IS USED BOTH FOR THE SHEET AND AS A TRIM ON THE CUSHIONS.

CENTRE LEFT ON THE SAME BED, THE GREEN GINGHAM HAS AGAIN BEEN USED FOR THE KICK-PLEAT VALANCE. THIS IS A DECORATIVE SOLUTION FOR DIVANS OR BEDS WITH STORAGE UNDERNEATH.

ABOVE IF YOU WANT AN ELABORATE FITTED HEADBOARD, IT IS IMPORTANT TO CONSIDER THE PLACEMENT OF PATTERN. HERE THE DIAMOND MOTIF IS POSITIONED CENTRALLY, WITH A ROPE BORDER OUTLINING THE SHAPE OF THE BOARD. THE COORDINATING FABRIC ON THE OUTSIDE EDGE IS PLEATED, SO EMPHASIZING ITS DECORATIVE NATURE. THE PLEATED VALANCE AND FRILLED BEDDING ALSO MIRROR THIS FEMININE STYLE. THE FORMALITY OF THE BED IS ACCENTUATED BY THE POSITIONING OF THE CUSHIONS.

FOCUS ON
FURNITURE

LEFT FURNITURE SHOULD
BE IN KEEPING WITH THE
MOOD AND STYLE OF A
ROOM, BE IT SIMPLE OR
GRAND. THIS WOVEN LLOYD
LOOM CHAIR AND PAINTED
TABLE HAVE A SUMMERY,
AIRY FEEL THAT SUITS THE
TONGUE-AND-GROOVE
WALLS AND PALE COLOURS
PERFECTLY.

The choice of furniture is crucial to the success of a room.
No other element plays such a vital role in determining how
well a scheme works, both practically and aesthetically.

And few elements offer such choice and versatility when we take the decision to transform a space.

The style, shape and proportions of a major piece of furniture have a strong influence on the look of a room. Consider, for example, the effect of a four-poster bed in a bedroom compared with that of two single beds. Style is also inherent in the materials and finish: a polished mahogany table will create a much more formal look than a white painted one.

Furniture provides a marvellous opportunity to juxtapose the old with the new; for example, a traditional armchair might be combined with a modern coffee table. The contrast of modern glass or metal surfaces with the rich patina of antique wood or the texture of worn leather greatly enriches an interior.

The layout of furniture in a room will determine whether it feels formal or relaxed, cosy or spacious. Individual items can be used as focal points to draw the eye and to alter the perception of a space. For instance, a tall, narrow bookcase will lead the eye upwards, creating an impression of height, while a low, wide bookcase will emphasize horizontal space.

No matter what style is chosen, furniture must always satisfy the functional needs of a room and those who use it. There is a wide range of options for seating, surfaces and storage, and it is important to choose items that offer the right mixture of practicality, flexibility and comfort.

Advice on selecting furniture for specific rooms can be found in Rooms for Living, pages 128–157. The following chapter offers guidance on assessing needs, choosing styles and placing furniture in a room.

ABOVE THE SHAPE OF
SEATING CAN SEND OUT
CLEAR MESSAGES ABOUT
COMFORT. IN THIS LIVING
ROOM, GENEROUSLY
UPHOLSTERED, WELL-
ROUNDED SEATS LOOK
PLUMP AND INVITING. THE
MATCHING FOOTSTOOL
ACCENTUATES THE RELAXED
ATMOSPHERE.

Furniture Needs

The best way to assess your requirements is to draw up a list detailing the seating, surfaces and storage needed to meet the practical needs of the room. At this point, disregard the items you already own. Now draw the items on the list onto a floor plan (see pages 14–15), allowing space for doors to open and for movement around the room. Assess your existing furniture in relation to the floor plan and the style and mood you are aiming for. You can then

LEFT IT IS NOT NECESSARY TO USE MATCHING CHAIRS IN A LIVING OR DINING ROOM. THIS ECLECTIC COLLECTION OF CANE, UPHOLSTERED AND LOOSE-COVERED PIECES WORK HAPPILY TOGETHER BECAUSE THEY HAVE BEEN KEPT WITHIN THE SAME FAMILY OF COLOURS.

decide whether to keep it, replace it or alter it in some way. For example, it might be worth keeping a sofa but changing the upholstery, painting an old dresser to give it new life, or adding a shelf to a cupboard for extra storage.

The floor plan will also give you the opportunity to rethink the arrangement of furniture. For example, a sofa and two chairs with a table in the middle is a classic combination, but you may prefer to have two sofas opposite each other or even to replace the sofa with armchairs to give you space for a bureau or bookcase.

ABOVE SOME PIECES OF FURNITURE, SUCH AS THIS FABULOUS WROUGHT-IRON DAY BED, HAVE MORE TO OFFER FROM A DECORATIVE POINT OF VIEW THAN A PRACTICAL ONE – USE THEM TO PROVIDE A FOCAL POINT WITHIN A ROOM.

ABOVE WHEN CHOOSING STORAGE FURNITURE CONSIDER WHETHER YOU WANT TO CONCEAL OR DISPLAY THE ITEMS WITHIN – THIS FREE-STANDING CUPBOARD IS AN ELEGANT WAY OF KEEPING THE KITCHEN TIDY.

BELOW THIS COUNTRY-STYLE CUPBOARD OFFERS A RANGE OF STORAGE OPTIONS IN A COMPACT BEDROOM. BEING A LIGHT COLOUR, IT DOES NOT DOMINATE THE SPACE.

Comfort

When choosing furniture that you sit on or lie on, such as sofas, chairs and beds, buy the best quality you can afford, with comfort high on your list of priorities. Comfort can mean different things to different people. Do you like to fall back into a squashy sofa or would you prefer to sit more upright with good back support? It is important to choose a mixture of furniture types, shapes and sizes to cater for the different people who will use the space and for the various activities that will take place there.

Unless you have a very spacious room, do not buy an extra-large sofa. Regardless of whether it is a two-seater or a three-seater sofa, only two people will feel comfortable sitting on it at any given time. When it comes to using sofas, three is definitely a crowd.

With sofas and armchairs, consider the amount of maintenance they require. Feather and down cushions on seating are soft and inviting, but they will need plumping up regularly. Quilted foam, on the other hand, bounces back into shape. Similarly, a sofa that has a tightly upholstered back needs much less maintenance than one with loose cushions.

Storage

To work out your storage requirements, think about the different activities for which the room is used. Built-in storage, such as alcove cupboards, looks elegant, but free-standing storage furniture can be moved if necessary so it offers greater flexibility. You can of course use a mixture of the two. Furniture that combines storage with another function is extremely useful, especially in a small space, for example coffee tables with shelves or drawers for magazines, or beds with drawers for storing bed linen.

Remember that furniture for storage should not just be functional. Consider its visual impact with as much care as you would any other item.

ABOVE THE WAY PIECES OF FURNITURE ARE JUXTAPOSED CAN CREATE AN INTERESTING STILL LIFE. THE ELEGANCE OF THIS TALL CUPBOARD, WHICH HOUSES A TV AND VIDEO, HAS BEEN EMPHASIZED BY A PAIR OF BALLOON-BACK CHAIRS.

OPPOSITE OPEN SHELVING IS ONE OF THE SIMPLEST AND LEAST EXPENSIVE FORMS OF STORAGE AND DISPLAY. HERE, MOULDING HAS BEEN USED TO FRAME SHELVES.

Furniture Style

When choosing any piece of furniture, be it a sofa, a bookcase, an armoire, a bureau or a chest, it must not only work well in terms of comfort or practicality, but should suit the style of the room and create a pleasing effect when juxtaposed with other items in the scheme.

Think about the key issues of shape, scale, colour and texture. Do you want furniture that is very simple and natural, such as cane; something hard-edged and smart, for example metal; a more rustic style, like stripped wood; or something with an element of luxury, such as lacquer?

Major pieces of furniture

The larger, more permanent items of furniture, such as sofas, dressers and armchairs, naturally have the greatest impact on the style of an interior. Particularly large or decorative pieces often become focal points. A wonderful dresser, for example, makes an eye-catching centrepiece in a kitchen. A glorious four-poster bed needs little else around it. Items such as these form an integral part of the design and need to be considered when deciding on the overall scheme.

These key pieces should always be chosen to suit the style and proportions of the internal architecture. If you have a low bedroom ceiling, for example, do not buy a bed that is boxy or too high. Try also to imagine the impact of the item's volume on the space. Using furniture that is very solid-looking, such as dark wooden pieces, can make a small room feel very crowded. Furniture made of glass, laminates, shiny metals, cane and light-coloured wood will lessen the effect of solidity and give an airier feel to a room. Seating need not always mean fully upholstered furniture. A rattan sofa with seat cushions will appear much less dense.

Finally, remember that less is often more: a few well-chosen and carefully placed items will maximize the light and space in a room, which is crucial to a feeling of relaxation and comfort. This will also allow individual pieces to stand out.

OPPOSITE
PIECES OF FURNITURE SHOULD WORK TOGETHER TO PRODUCE A HARMONIOUS BLEND OF TEXTURE, COLOUR AND DECORATIVE STYLE. THE WELL-TRAVELLED, ECLECTIC TONE OF THIS COMFORTABLE LIVING ROOM HAS BEEN SET BY THE ANTIQUE INDIAN CUPBOARD, THE LARGE COFFEE TABLE AND THE MANY BOOKS AND ACCESSORIES. PATCHES OF RED AGAINST THE NEUTRAL TONES ADD FURTHER STIMULATION AND BRING OUT THE RICHNESS OF THE WOOD.

TOP RIGHT
USE FURNITURE TO CREATE INTERESTING TABLEAUX AROUND THE HOUSE. THIS RUSTIC BENCH SCATTERED WITH CUSHIONS MAKES A HOMELY ADDITION TO A STONE PASSAGEWAY.

CENTRE RIGHT
SEARCH JUNK SHOPS AND SALVAGE YARDS FOR PIECES THAT MAY BE PAST THEIR FUNCTIONAL BEST BUT STILL HAVE DECORATIVE APPEAL. THE DISTRESSED SURFACE OF THIS METAL CHAIR GIVES IT VISUAL INTEREST.

BOTTOM RIGHT
A RAY OF SUNLIGHT THROWS THE WONDERFUL NATURAL TEXTURE OF THIS WICKER CHAIR INTO SHARP RELIEF. THE CUSHION AND THROW NOT ONLY ADD COMFORT BUT CREATE A PLEASING CONTRAST WITH THE WOVEN SURFACE.

Smaller items

The smaller items of furniture offer great scope in terms of both style and practicality. These are the pieces to add once all the major elements are in place, and that are enjoyable to collect over time from antique shops, auctions and markets. They are also the most portable items of furniture and can be moved around a room or a home to revitalize different areas. In fact one of the simplest ways of transforming an interior is to spend a few hours moving tables, chairs and chests to different positions.

The list of smaller pieces is a long one and includes occasional tables, butlers' trays, coffee tables, sofa-end tables and side tables that can be used for decorative displays or to extend surface areas when entertaining. Occasional chairs, such as wood, wicker or Lloyd Loom, are not only practical but add another decorative layer to a room. Children's chairs are useful at the side of a sofa, armchair or bed as a surface for books and magazines, or to hold piles of towels in a bathroom. They can either be left as plain wood or painted to complement a colour scheme.

Decorative screens are useful for dividing space, concealing awkward areas, or creating a more intimate atmosphere in a large room. Whether painted, made of textured wood or fabric-covered, they also add interest to an interior.

Large baskets are very versatile – they can be placed at the end of a bed to store seasonal bed linen and blankets, kept in a hall for gloves, hats and scarves, or used in a family room for games and videos. They also bring pleasing natural colours and textures to a room.

Finally there are the more purely decorative pieces of furniture such as a rocking horse that stands in a hall or a grandfather clock whose chimes bring back happy memories of childhood – such items bring individuality and character to a home.

OPPOSITE
FURNITURE NEED NOT BE EXPENSIVE, PROVIDED YOU ARE HAPPY TO MIX OLD WITH NEW, BARE WOOD WITH PAINTED, URBAN WITH RUSTIC. DON'T BE AFRAID TO PICK UP A PAINTBRUSH AND CUSTOMIZE A PROMISING PIECE FOR YOUR OWN HOME. THIS SIMPLE KITCHEN TABLE HAS BEEN CHOSEN FOR ITS DOG-EARED CHARM AND HAS BEEN PAINTED BLUE TO COMPLEMENT THE KITCHEN CHAIRS. CHECKED CUSHIONS EMPHASIZE THE INFORMAL ATMOSPHERE.

BELOW SOMETIMES IT IS BETTER TO CHOOSE DESIGNS THAT HAVE A TRANSPARENT QUALITY. THIS DOES NOT MEAN USING ONLY GLASS OR PERSPEX, BUT CHOOSING PIECES – SUCH AS THIS SLIM FOLD-AWAY TABLE – THAT ALLOW THE WALLS TO BE SEEN.

ABOVE FURNITURE SHOULD SUIT YOUR LIFESTYLE, NOT VICE VERSA. IF YOU LIKE TO ENTERTAIN A COUPLE OF FRIENDS ONE EVENING AND FOURTEEN THE NEXT, TAKE A LATERAL APPROACH TO DINING ARRANGEMENTS. THESE MATCHING TABLES CAN BE PUSHED TOGETHER WHEN NUMBERS DEMAND. THE RUNNERS GIVE AN ILLUSION OF CONTINUITY.

One of the simplest ways of transforming an interior is to spend a few hours moving tables, chairs and chests to different positions.

TRANSFORMATIONS

STYLE FILE

Style is often equated with fashion but it means much more than this. Many diverse elements are needed to create a home and imposing a style enables us to bring them together to form a cohesive and pleasing whole. A style also gives a home its distinctive character, one that reflects the lives and personalities of those who live in it.

The inspiration for a style can come from anywhere. It could be a favorite colour, a treasured collection or a magnificent piece of furniture. Some styles are inspired by the landscape – a seaside location, for example, may suggest the use of bleached colours, shell fabrics and driftwood sculptures. Others have their origins in the architecture of the house or apartment, or the interests of the owner. However, a style should not be adopted for its visual effect alone. Its success will depend on how well it suits your way of life.

On a purely practical level, choosing a style makes the task of transforming a home that much easier. With so many decisions to make about colour and pattern, furniture and fabrics, and so many choices available, it is important to establish the boundaries to work within.

This section takes four different styles – Simple, Pretty, Comfortable and Decorative – and shows how to create them in your own home. Each has a classic appeal, but they are by no means the only choices. If you want to interpret one in a different way, or develop one of your own making, there is an important lesson to note: every element of the room, from the flooring material to the flowers, should be chosen to harmonize with the overall look. Paying attention to details, large and small, will enable you to create a successful, unified style.

ABOVE THE INSPIRATION FOR A STYLE CAN COME FROM ONE KEY PIECE THAT ANCHORS ALL THE OTHER COLOURS AND PATTERNS IN A ROOM TOGETHER. THE WONDERFUL PRINTED QUILT SHOWN HERE WAS THE FOUNDATION FOR THIS SIMPLE COUNTRY BEDROOM WITH ITS TONGUE-AND-GROOVE DADO AND PRETTY PAINTED BED. OTHER COLOURS HAVE BEEN KEPT FAIRLY MINIMAL, SO THE EYE IS FOCUSED ON THE BED ITSELF.

OPPOSITE FABRICS ARE CENTRAL TO THE STYLE OF A ROOM AS THEY SEND OUT MESSAGES NOT ONLY THROUGH COLOUR AND PATTERN, BUT ALSO THROUGH TEXTURE AND TRIMS. THE CUSHIONS ON THIS BED, FOR EXAMPLE, EPITOMIZE ROMANCE WITH THEIR PASTEL SHADES, SCALLOPED EDGES, APPLIQUÉ WORK AND RIBBON BRAIDS. THE COTTON VOILE BED DRAPE IS SIMILARLY SOFT AND EVOCATIVE.

Simple

Simple has been a key word in design in recent years. It is not to be confused with minimal, as it is much softer and more comfortable than that term implies.

The Simple canvas should have few colours and plenty of natural surfaces. It is enough to choose three shades of white for walls and woodwork. However, introducing stronger highlight colours, such as taupe, sand or oatmeal, or even reds, blues and aquas, adds impact while retaining a clean, uncomplicated look.

Think of natural textures when it comes to flooring. Sanded floorboards that are varnished, bleached, painted or limed make a good backdrop for seagrass mats bound with linen. Or cover the whole floor in coir, sisal or jute. Rugs such as kilims can be used to add colour, pattern and texture.

Window treatments should be tailored – wooden shutters, pinoleum blinds, plain or linen roller blinds or unlined linen curtains are all ideal. If you decide to use a pattern, choose a faded floral, a figurative toile, checks or ticking stripes.

Complement the unbroken lines of the room with furniture in classic shapes, either modern pieces or finds from auctions. Use painted furniture for a smart simple look, or distressed wood for a more rustic atmosphere.

Create a space that flows calmly, with highlight colours to provide vitality and interest. Add texture through wicker baskets, wooden artefacts and hand-made ceramics. Nature is important in the simple interior – use flowers in single varieties.

OPPOSITE NEUTRALS WITH A TOUCH OF COLOUR CREATE A SIMPLE BUT SMART LOOK. HERE THE RICH WOOD OF THE TABLE IS COMPLEMENTED BY THE RUSSETS IN THE RUG AND THE PINKISH HUES OF THE UPHOLSTERY AND BLIND. ALL ARE SET AGAINST A QUIET BACKGROUND OF CREAM WALLS AND NATURAL LINENS.

ABOVE COLOURS ARE KEPT TO A MINIMUM IN THIS ROOM IN ORDER TO THROW MORE EMPHASIS ONTO TEXTURES SUCH AS THE OPEN-WEAVE LINEN CURTAINS AND POLISHED OAK CHAIRS. APPLE RED HAS BEEN INTRODUCED THROUGH FABRIC, BUT IT IS THE WOODEN BOWL AND CREAM POTTERY THAT DRAW THE EYE.

RIGHT LINEN LOOSE COVERS
EMPHASIZE THE FORM OF
THESE BALLOON-BACK
CHAIRS WHILE MINIMIZING
COLOUR AND PATTERN.
ONLY THE BLUE OVERCLOTH
HAS A PURELY DECORATIVE
FUNCTION. THE SIMPLE
THEME IS CONTINUED IN
THE NATURAL CARPET AND
THE CHOICE OF PLAIN
WOODEN SHUTTERS FOR
THE WINDOW.

LEFT BARE BOARDS AND
NEUTRAL COLOURS ARE THE
PERFECT BEGINNING FOR A
CALM, QUIET SCHEME. THE
MIX OF OLD AND NEW IS A
RELEVANT THEME, WITH THE
SMALL ANTIQUE OAK DESK
AND CHAIR COMPLEMENTED
BY AN OLD BLANKET ON THE
ARMCHAIR. THE LINEN
ROMAN BLIND AND
MATELASSÉ UPHOLSTERY
FABRIC ENHANCE THE
CLEAN, GRAPHIC LINES.

RIGHT WINDOWS ARE A KEY
CONSIDERATION WHEN
CREATING THE SIMPLE LOOK.
IF CURTAINS ARE CHOSEN AS
OPPOSED TO BLINDS, THEY
SHOULD BE MODEST IN
COLOUR, PATTERN AND
DESIGN. UNLINED COTTON
THAT HANGS STRAIGHT TO
THE FLOOR, AS SHOWN
HERE, IS A GOOD CHOICE.
HEADINGS TOO SHOULD BE
MINIMAL – ONES THAT CLIP
ONTO AN UNOBTRUSIVE
POLE LOOK BEST.

LEFT EMPHASIZE TEXTURE
BY CREATING CONTRASTS.
HERE THE DISTRESSED
SURFACE OF AN OLD CHAIR
IS JUXTAPOSED WITH A
SOFT, FRILLY CUSHION FOR
AN INTERESTING EFFECT.
THEIR MATT FINISH DIFFERS
IN TURN FROM THE SHINY
WOODEN BOWL AND THE
GLOSSY CHERRIES.

THIS PAGE AND OPPOSITE ALTHOUGH IT IS USUALLY ASSOCIATED WITH VERY SOFT COLOURS, PRETTY CAN ALSO HAVE A MUCH FRESHER INTERPRETATION. IN THIS SUNNY BREAKFAST AREA, BOLD BLUE AND YELLOW HAVE BEEN USED TO CREATE AN INVIGORATING SCHEME. CHECKS AND STRIPES ALWAYS WORK WELL TOGETHER, BUT THE CURTAIN DESIGN – STRIPS OF CONTRASTING GINGHAMS – IS AN UNUSUAL WAY OF COMBINING THE TWO. SIMPLE BENTWOOD CHAIRS HAVE BEEN PAINTED BLUE TO COMPLEMENT FABRICS AND CHINA. FRESH BLOOMS FROM THE GARDEN PROVIDE THE PERFECT FINISHING TOUCH.

Pretty

If you want a romantic look with a timeless appeal, choose Pretty. Everything in the Pretty room is soft to the touch and pleasing to the eye. For colours, think of pinks, greens, corals, aquas, peaches and yellows. Or go slightly bolder with cornflower blues and egg yolk yellows. Team these with off-whites or creams – brilliant white will be too stark.

Apply these shades as either a flat paint finish or a decorative effect, such as stencilling or sponging. Wallpaper is an easy way of achieving the pretty look. It can be used as an all-over design or as a border against a painted surface.

Choose carpets in soft, plain colours; place needlework or rag rugs on top for added interest. Painted bare boards are also appropriate for this look, so long as there is a rug underfoot for warmth.

The pretty room suits curtains made in gingham checks, large florals or delicate motifs; for a truly romantic look add frilled or scalloped edges. Old or new embroidered fabrics and floaty voiles look fabulous too. Use tie-backs to emphasize the curves of fabric, and echo these in the shapes of furniture, headboards and cushions. Choose rounded lamp bases and pleated or embroidered shades. Trimmings are vital, so embellish curtains and other furnishings with ribbon, braid, fringing or tassels.

Antique or painted furniture works best. The latter could feature patterns such as trailing florals or leaves that echo a motif in the wallpaper or fabric.

Suitable accessories include blue-and-white china, decorative photo frames and bunches of freshly picked flowers. Scent is important in the pretty room: sweet peas or lilies-of-the-valley are the perfect choice.

BELOW FABRICS ARE THE IDEAL WAY OF INTRODUCING SOFT COLOURS AND ROMANTIC PATTERNS. HERE, VOILE DRAPES FRAME A BED THAT IS BEAUTIFULLY DRESSED IN TICKING STRIPES, PRINTED FLORALS AND WHITE LINEN.

BELOW AND BOTTOM BLUE WALLS AND CREAMY UPHOLSTERY MAKE AN IDEAL BACKDROP FOR ROSE-COLOURED FLORALS AND RED TIE-BACKS. THE DECORATIVE CUSHIONS ARE A MIXTURE OF NEW PRINTS AND ANTIQUE REMNANTS.

ABOVE THERE SHOULD ALWAYS BE ONE VERY DECORATIVE FABRIC IN THE PRETTY SCHEME, FROM WHICH OTHERS CAN BE CHOSEN TO COORDINATE. THE SOFT PINK AND GREEN FLORAL FABRIC USED FOR THIS BEDSPREAD IS THE ANCHOR FOR EVERYTHING FROM THE SHEER BED CURTAIN TO THE SPRIGGED PILLOW.

OPPOSITE THE ORNATE DESIGN OF THIS PAINTED CHAIR IS THE PERFECT FOIL FOR THE ROMANTIC ROUND CUSHIONS. EACH CUSHION CAN BE DIFFERENT, SO LONG AS THE SAME COLOUR PALETTE IS USED. CHECKS OR STRIPES WITH FLORALS WORK WELL; USE ANOTHER DESIGN FOR CONTRAST PIPING.

Comfortable

The comfortable room epitomizes informality and ease. Strong, simple colours, bold patterns, rounded shapes and natural textures add up to a relaxed look that is rich in character.

Of all the styles described, this is the most flexible. Walls can be kept neutral to make seasonal changes easier, or painted in soft colours that inject personality and provide a contrasting background to furniture in more vibrant tones.

Floors can be hard, such as varnished boards, but if so they should be covered in patterned rugs to provide a soft and quiet surface to walk upon. If you prefer a fitted carpet, opt for a textured one that can itself be covered with a rug.

Choose classic window treatments such as full-length curtains with informal headings or roller or Roman blinds. Large-scale patterns are important so exploit the graphic qualities of big checks and wide stripes. If upholstery fabrics are kept plain, use pattern on cushions, rugs or curtains.

Furniture should look as inviting as possible, so buy generous sofas and chairs that you can sink into. Hard edges and sharp corners should be kept to a minimum. When it comes to furniture styles, choose an informal, eclectic mix, from dark wood to painted, rattan to upholstered. What matters is that the pieces complement each other.

Lighting is a key component of the Comfortable interior. Walking into an over-bright room is not relaxing, but there should be enough light to read or play games by. This means having plenty of lamps and fitting dimmer switches to overhead lights.

As far as accessories are concerned, anything goes – so long as it adds to the mood. This is the place for stacks of books, well-thumbed magazines, unusual objects, or hurricane lamps for candles. Use exotic foliage plants and simple bunches of flowers to enhance the comfortable atmosphere.

ABOVE LEFT AND OPPOSITE A COMFORTABLE LOOK ALLOWS YOU TO BRING IN UNUSUAL TOUCHES SUCH AS THE OARS USED FOR CURTAIN POLES IN THIS LIVING ROOM OR THE COLLECTION OF CORALS AND STONES ON THE COFFEE TABLE.

BELOW LEFT THE INFORMAL LAYOUT OF THIS KITCHEN IS PERFECT FOR A FAMILY HOME. COMFORTABLE CHAIRS AND A COSY AGA GIVE THE BARN-LIKE SPACE AN INTIMATE ATMOSPHERE.

BELOW THIS INFORMAL WICKER FURNITURE HAS BEEN GIVEN EXTRA COMFORT WITH PLUMP CUSHIONS ON THE SEATS AND BACKS. PATCHES OF PIMENTO RED CREATE A VIBRANT ATMOSPHERE.

BELOW THE MAGNIFICENT DESIGN AND SUMPTUOUS SHADES OF AN ORIENTAL CARPET MAKE THE PERFECT FOUNDATION FOR A COMFORTABLE ROOM. THE TIME-WORN WOOD AND TEXTURED UPHOLSTERY FABRIC HARMONIZE BEAUTIFULLY.

OPPOSITE AND ABOVE WARM COLOURS AND COSY FURNITURE CREATE A FRIENDLY AMBIENCE IN THIS COUNTRY LIVING ROOM. BOOKS, COLLECTIONS AND INTERESTING MEMENTOS ADD TO ITS TIMELESS QUALITY. THE LOW, DEEP, CHENILLE-COVERED SOFA DEMONSTRATES THE KEY ROLE PLAYED BY FURNITURE SHAPE IN EVOKING A RELAXED MOOD.

ABOVE THE COMFORTABLE LOOK CAN BE CONTINUED OUTDOORS BY APPLYING THE SAME CRITERIA OF ROUNDED SHAPES AND INVITING COLOURS AND TEXTURES, AS ILLUSTRATED BY THESE RATTAN CHAIRS.

Decorative

What characterizes the decorative look is a considered and cohesive use of pattern and texture. Walls can be either kept plain as a foil to other patterns or used to set the tone with an over-scaled wallpaper such as damask. Colour is used confidently, but is often restricted to a few complementary shades so their impact is all the stronger.

Woodblock floors overlaid with richly patterned rugs for comfort work well with this look. Alternatively, decorative designs can be stencilled onto varnished floorboards. Highly patterned carpets are also suitable.

For window treatments, choose curtains with decorative headings and sumptuous trims, or simple curtains in luxurious fabrics such as unlined silk or taffeta, chenilles or velvets.

As well as mixing different patterns, vary the scales too. Using coordinated ranges of wallpaper and fabric makes this easier. Sumptuous textures add to the feeling of luxury, as do antique textiles made into cushions, or pieces of needlepoint used to cover small items of furniture. Mix paisleys with chenilles and decorative cottons with linens.

Furniture can be old, new or a mixture. The key is to use opulent materials such as rich woods or glass. Reflections add another layer of interest, so position mirrors well, possibly with candles in front of them. Accessorize with interesting objects such as antique boxes, decorative baskets, porcelain bowls, coloured glass and silver photo frames.

TO ACHIEVE A SUCCESSFUL DECORATIVE LOOK CHOOSE FABRICS IN COMPLEMENTARY COLOURS AND USE THEM IN AN IMAGINATIVE WAY. A DUCK-INSPIRED FABRIC IS THE ANCHOR FOR THE REST OF THIS CONFIDENT SCHEME, BRINGING TOGETHER EVERYTHING FROM THE TRIM ON THE BLIND TO THE SKIRT ON THE CHAIR.

BELOW A DECORATIVE ELEMENT CAN BE INTRODUCED THROUGH FURNITURE AND DETAILS AS WELL AS WALLS AND FABRIC. THIS CARVED INDIAN CUPBOARD IS THE FOCAL POINT OF THE ROOM; BUT ATTENTION IS ALSO DRAWN TOWARDS THE WOODEN ARTEFACTS IN BOWLS AND THE TEXTURED BASKETS. BOLD CHECKED BLINDS ACCENTUATE THE RICHNESS OF THE COLOUR.

ABOVE IF YOU WANT TO TAKE A MORE RESTRAINED APPROACH TO THE DECORATIVE LOOK, USE NEUTRALS AS A BASE BUT TEAM THEM WITH A RICH COLOUR OR STRONG PATTERN. IN THIS COOL LIVING ROOM, THE MAGNIFICENT CARPET IS ALL THAT IS NEEDED TO LIFT THE SCHEME.

ABOVE STRONG COLOURS NEED ONLY BE USED IN SMALL QUANTITIES TO BRING VISUAL EXCITEMENT TO A ROOM. THE SCARLET CLOTH ON THIS CHAIR IS A CONTRAST TO THE CREAMY UPHOLSTERY FABRIC USED ELSEWHERE, BUT IT ECHOES THE RED-TRIMMED CURTAINS PERFECTLY.

RIGHT THIS BLUE-AND-WHITE BEDSPREAD HAS PROVIDED INSPIRATION FOR EVERYTHING IN THE ROOM, FROM LAMPSHADES AND BLIND TO FOOTSTOOL AND CUSHIONS.

RIGHT BY KEEPING TO A SINGLE FAMILY OF COLOURS, SUCH AS THE BLUES OF THIS LIVING ROOM, IT IS POSSIBLE TO COMBINE MANY TYPES OF PATTERN. EVEN THE STRIKING GEOMETRY OF THE RUG WORKS WELL AMONG THE FLORALS, STRIPES AND CHECKS.

PAY ATTENTION TO THE FINISH OF INDIVIDUAL ITEMS AS WELL AS TO
HOW THE WHOLE SCHEME WORKS. THE WOODEN BUTTONS ON THIS
CUSHION, FOR EXAMPLE, ADD ANOTHER LAYER OF INTEREST TO THE
DRESSING OF THE BED. COMBINATIONS OF OLD AND NEW FABRICS
ALSO BRING CHARACTER TO THE ROOM.

ROOMS FOR LIVING

Successful decorating means understanding the core principles of space, light, colour and texture, and then applying them to specific rooms. It is the use of a space that has the biggest influence on the elements chosen for a scheme.

In other words, it is easy to decide that you would like a blue room or a pretty room, but it is not until you have considered all the issues relating to use and comfort, and how each room or space interacts with the next, that you can make the right decisions about flooring, wall coverings, window treatments, upholstery, furniture, lamps and accessories. The demands of a hall are quite different to those of a bathroom, just as a dining room requires a very different approach to a bedroom.

In this chapter, the principles explained in the previous chapters are related to the key rooms in a home. In each case, it is a question of assessing the functional requirements of the space and those who will be using it, and deciding what is needed practically to make it work well.

Today we often want individual rooms to fulfil more than one role, such as a kitchen that is used for informal dining or a living room that includes a work area. However, the same criteria for choosing furniture, storage and lighting apply to these spaces as they do to separate, dedicated rooms. The only difference is that the overall decorative scheme needs to be designed in such a way that the various areas within the space are well defined but are in sympathy with one another.

What you decide is right for your home is an entirely personal matter. There is an infinite number of options when it comes to tackling any room, large or small. The best way to use this chapter is as a catalyst for your own ideas.

OPPOSITE A WELCOMING SEAT, A BEAUTIFULLY TEXTURED FLOOR AND A FORMAL WALL DISPLAY TRANSFORM A HALL FROM A PASSAGE TO WALK THROUGH INTO AN AREA TO LINGER IN. THE MIRROR IS CLEVERLY PLACED TO BRING LIGHT INTO THE SPACE.

ABOVE THE STYLE OF A ROOM IS OFTEN SET BY ONE MAJOR PIECE OF FURNITURE. THE BLUE RANGE SHOWN HERE IS MUCH MORE THAN A COOKING SOURCE – IT IS THE SOURCE OF COLOUR INSPIRATION, THE BACKDROP TO CHINA AND AN IMPORTANT FOCAL POINT WITHIN THE ROOM.

Entrances and Halls

All the ingredients in a hall – from what visitors feel underfoot and stop to look at on the walls to the scents that greet them and the light they step into – combine to create an abiding first impression of a home. A hall is also a transitional space, linking the outside world with the interior and connecting one room with the next.

The first thing to consider is whether the hall needs an area where people stop to take off their coats or wipe their shoes. Some houses have porches for this purpose, but it is easy to simulate the same area by laying a different floor close to the front door. A square metre of tiles or natural matting is not only functional but separates one part of the hall from the rest.

Next decide whether the hall should act simply as a passageway, leading calmly through to other rooms, or whether it should be decorated as a room in its own right.

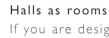

Halls as passageways

This option means visually extending the hall right into the home. Floors are a good way of achieving continuity from one space to the next. This is why many people choose one shade of carpet for their entire ground floor, or lay hardwood floors throughout.

Wall colour is another way of linking rooms. This does not mean using the same decorative scheme throughout, but it could mean echoing the wall colour from the hall in the architrave of the living room, or choosing colours from the same family. It is best to work from a palette of harmonious shades for a transitional space.

This type of hall should lead the eye forwards to the rooms beyond. This means positioning focal points such as paintings, mirrors or furniture at the far end of the hall. Suitably shaped paintings can be hung high over doorways as signposts to beckon people forwards.

Halls as rooms

If you are designing the hall as a room then you may want to emphasize its decorative qualities. Because this is a space you pass through rather than sitting in for any length of time, you can be bolder here and use stronger colours, for example, both on walls and floors. You could also use the hall as a gallery-style space for paintings or decorative objects. If you do not have anything suitable with which to cover such a large expanse of wall, use a richly patterned wallpaper.

If space allows, a hall can be made even more comfortable by adding a sofa or a pair of bookcases.

Lighting and storage

Whichever approach you take, do not overlook the importance of lighting. The light should be bright enough to ensure that the stairs are safe and that you can find keys and other items easily, but not so bright as to create an unwelcoming atmosphere. Provided the ceiling is high enough, a hall is the ideal location for an elegant overhead light such as a chandelier.

Storage is another key consideration. There must be plenty of room for hanging coats and hats, and places to leave wet umbrellas and outdoor shoes. An antique coat or umbrella stand adds a decorative touch.

THIS PAGE
EVEN UNCOVERED STAIRS
CAN BE DECORATIVE.
PAINTED WITH TOUGH
FLOOR PAINT, THIS
STAIRCASE HAS BEEN
GIVEN A CLEVER RUNNER
EFFECT THAT MATCHES
THE WALL SHADE.

OPPOSITE ABOVE
ENTRANCES AND DOORS
PROVIDE THE FIRST SIGN
OF WHAT TO EXPECT FROM
A HOME. THIS HOUSE IN
NEW ENGLAND HAS AN
IMPRESSIVE DOORWAY,
WHICH IS SOFTENED BY
THE HOMELY WREATH AND
GARDEN ACCOUTREMENTS.

OPPOSITE BELOW
HALLS ARE ESSENTIALLY
TRAFFIC ROUTES BETWEEN
THE DIFFERENT AREAS OF
A HOME. COLOUR CAN BE
USED TO CREATE IMPACT
AND TO LEAD THE EYE
FORWARDS INTO THE
INTERIOR, AS HERE.

Relaxing

While it goes without saying that every room in your home should make you feel relaxed, it is important to have at least one area that is entirely dedicated to your ease and comfort. It might be a place to watch television or listen to music; to read a book or pursue a hobby. This is a sanctuary to head for after a busy day, where you will feel rested the moment you walk through the door.

This space is usually, but not always, the living room. A living room today needs to fulfil a variety of roles, from family activities to formal entertaining. A place for relaxing, however, may be anywhere from a sofa in a kitchen to an armchair in a study, from a quiet corner in a conservatory to a wicker chair on a terrace. It might be an oasis for you alone, or one you share with others.

Whatever form it takes, the key words to remember when designing a room for relaxing are practicality and comfort. Practicality does not just relate to the choice of materials. It also means ensuring the room has the best kind of lighting for what you want to do there, that it is warm enough, and that it contains the right amount and type of furniture and storage.

Choose flooring that is comfortable to walk on, even when barefoot. Deep wool carpet is luxurious, an invitation to kick off your shoes, but in warmer weather it is lovely to feel a cool surface underfoot. One solution is to lay a hard floor first then put soft unfitted carpets or rugs over the top, which can be easily removed in summer. Rich patterns on rugs will add to the impression of visual comfort. Another option

ABOVE THE LAYOUT OF FURNITURE MAKES A VITAL CONTRIBUTION TO THE ATMOSPHERE OF A LIVING ROOM. CHOOSE AND POSITION CHAIRS TO CATER FOR DIFFERENT ACTIVITIES, SUCH AS THE ARMCHAIR SET BACK IN THIS ROOM FOR READING BY THE WINDOW.

OPPOSITE A DECORATIVE MIRROR PROVIDES A FOCAL POINT IN A ROOM. THIS ROUND GILT DESIGN CREATES AN ATTRACTIVE TABLEAU ABOVE THE ANTIQUE CHEST, COMPLEMENTED BY THE SYMMETRICAL ARRANGEMENT OF MINIATURE BAY TREES.

Decoration

In a room for relaxing everything should please the senses of sight and touch. Generally speaking, it is best to opt for a palette of favourite colours, rather than experimenting wildly. Walking into a space decorated in harmonious colours will immediately make you feel at ease. Given the amount of time we spend in such rooms it is vital that the colour scheme works well by natural and artificial light.

Walking into a room decorated in harmonious colours will immediately make you feel at ease.

is to use natural flooring, for example seagrass or jute, which is practical and textural and conveys a feeling of simplicity. If you have children, a hardwood floor with washable rugs is a sensible option.

The window treatment is also important. Layering curtains with blinds will give you the most flexibility. Luxurious curtains are wonderful in winter because they create a feeling of being enveloped in fabric, protected from the cold outside. In summer, tie them back and use either simple blinds or sheer curtains.

Furniture and storage

When choosing furniture, again make comfort the priority. Decide which items are needed to suit the different activities in the room, for example a deep sofa for curling up in, a wing armchair for reading and an upright chair and a desk for writing letters. If space allows, try to include more than one seating area in the room. As well as creating a focal point where people can gather to talk, such as the space around a fire, you could also have an area for games, such as a pair of chairs next to a window seat.

THIS PAGE AND OPPOSITE COLOUR IS ONE OF THE MOST POWERFUL TOOLS FOR CREATING A RELAXED ATMOSPHERE. HERE, A CREAM SOFA AND RED ARMCHAIRS COMBINE WITH NEUTRAL WALLS AND A RICHLY PATTERNED RUG TO INVEST THE ROOM WITH A FEELING OF EASE. EVERYTHING, FROM THE PLACEMENT OF FURNITURE TO THE SIMPLE BUNCH OF FLOWERS, WORKS TOGETHER TO MAKE THIS A WELCOMING RETREAT. THE USE OF PATTERN IN THE ROOM IS BOTH DECORATIVE AND COSY. THE THROWS, CUSHIONS AND WINDOW-SEAT COVERS ARE UNIFIED BY SHADES OF RED, COLOURS THAT WERE INSPIRED BY THE PAISLEY SHAWL ON THE BACK OF THE SOFA.

Do not feel that the major items of furniture must match. Use a mixture of old and new pieces, or fully upholstered items and occasional chairs, to create interesting juxtapositions. For example, an old worn leather armchair will bring character to a room and make a pleasing contrast to a modern sofa. What is important is that the colours, shapes and textures of the different pieces work well together.

When it comes to choosing upholstery fabrics, there are plenty of materials you can use that will emphasize comfort. Try a mixture of quilted fabrics, old and new items, and soft textiles such as brushed cottons, wool, felt and chenille. Using loose covers on sofas and chairs and buying oversized cushions will give a less formal look to a room. Double-sided throws, with hard-wearing linen-and-wool on one side and cashmere on the other, are a simple way of adding an element of luxury.

Occasional tables and low coffee tables should be placed within easy reach of sofas and chairs for books or glasses. Footstools will encourage people to put their feet up and relax. Small tables are the ideal place to create a display of eye-catching objects, and to introduce colour, texture, scale and scent. A lamp will add height to the arrangement and illuminate the other items on the table.

If the room is used for entertaining, one of the most important ingredients is sufficient seating. As well as providing enough seats for the number of guests, make sure the seats are positioned in such a way that visitors feel they can sit anywhere. Furniture should also be arranged so that people can converse easily. This applies just as much to entertaining outdoors as it does to indoor functions. Occasional chairs at each side of the fireplace look elegant and can be rearranged when necessary. Window seats, fender seats and decorative chairs also provide extra seating should the need arise. Side tables are invaluable for entertaining as they provide additional surfaces for glasses, plates, serving dishes and extra cutlery.

Storage is an important consideration in a room that has to meet the needs of a diverse range of activities, which might include reading, listening to music, watching television or playing board games. Either wall-mounted or free-standing shelves are essential for storing favourite books, magazines and CDs. Make shelves look as attractive as possible by using wicker baskets or decorative boxes for storage arranged in a pleasing way.

A cupboard or a chest of drawers is invaluable for storing anything that you may not want to display, such as toys, games or videos. It also makes sense to have at least one item, for example a large basket, a blanket chest or an ottoman, into which you can put an accumulation of clutter if you need to tidy up in a hurry.

Lighting and accessories

A room for relaxing requires a well-designed and flexible lighting scheme. Because the space must cater to such a variety of activities, it is important to create several layers of lighting, including downlighters or table lamps for reading or writing, uplighters for atmosphere, and display lighting for illuminating bookshelves, pictures or focal points. Position floor and table lamps so that they are evenly distributed around the room and assess their effect from different viewpoints, including seats.

When choosing accessories, remember that a room for relaxing should express the personality of you and anyone else who uses it. A family room often becomes cluttered with well-thumbed books and magazines. This is a place to display items that have a special significance for you and your family.

An elegant living room, on the other hand, calls for a much more disciplined approach. Accessories need to be carefully chosen and placed to create a calm, quiet atmosphere.

Whatever form your room for relaxing takes, do not forget the importance of freshly cut, deliciously scented flowers, which will greatly enhance the feeling of welcome and comfort.

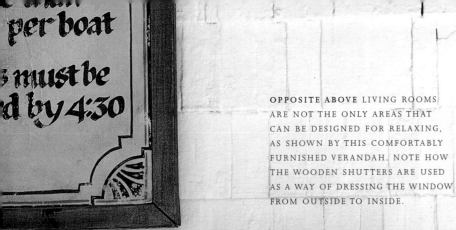

OPPOSITE ABOVE LIVING ROOMS ARE NOT THE ONLY AREAS THAT CAN BE DESIGNED FOR RELAXING, AS SHOWN BY THIS COMFORTABLY FURNISHED VERANDAH. NOTE HOW THE WOODEN SHUTTERS ARE USED AS A WAY OF DRESSING THE WINDOW FROM OUTSIDE TO INSIDE.

OPPOSITE BELOW THIS SPACE IS MUCH MORE OF AN EXTENSION OF THE HOUSE THAN A GARDEN ROOM. COLOURS AND TEXTURES, SUCH AS THE SLIGHTLY DISTRESSED SURFACE OF THE TABLE, COMBINE TO ACCENTUATE ITS INFORMAL ATMOSPHERE.

THIS PAGE BLUE AND YELLOW IS A CLASSIC COLOUR COMBINATION, SIGNIFYING WARMTH, SUN AND EASY LIVING – JUST THE QUALITIES NEEDED FOR AN OUTDOOR LIVING ROOM.

Cooking

One of the most important design trends of recent years has been the way that kitchens have become the heart of the home; not just places for preparing and eating food, but valuable living spaces in their own right.

Because of this, a kitchen needs to be considered on many different levels. Cooking is the primary activity and this demands an efficient use of space. Begin by thinking about how often you cook and the kinds of meals you are most likely to prepare. If cooking for you is more likely to mean heating up pre-prepared meals than cooking intricate recipes, a microwave might be more important than an Aga. If, on the other hand, you are an enthusiastic cook, then you will not only need a generous-sized oven and hob, but enough storage space for a battery of utensils and implements.

Planning the space

When designing a kitchen, follow the example of professionals and begin by drawing a floor plan (see pages 14–15). Remember the importance of the 'work triangle'. This is the invisible line drawn between the three main cooking zones of sink, hob or oven, and fridge. Ideally, no two areas should be more than a double arm span apart or so close to each other that they constrict freedom of movement. For safety reasons, try to avoid allowing traffic routes through the triangle.

Consider also the other activities that take place in your kitchen. A generously sized kitchen table is the perfect place to do homework, write letters or read a newspaper. And when you invite friends round for a meal, this is a natural place for them to gather while you cook.

Each of these activities will have a bearing on the materials chosen, the amount of storage needed and the type of lighting required.

LEFT ABOVE REGARDLESS OF THE STYLE, A KITCHEN MUST WORK FROM A PRACTICAL POINT OF VIEW. A DECENT-SIZED WORKTOP, FOR EXAMPLE, IS VITAL, WHETHER YOU OPT FOR SMART STEEL AND WENGE OR CUSTOMIZE YOUR OWN FROM A DISCARDED PIECE OF TIMBER. KEEP UTENSILS THAT ARE IN DAILY USE, SUCH AS CHOPPING BOARDS, KNIVES AND WOODEN SPOONS, CLOSE TO THE AREA IN WHICH THEY ARE USED, AS HERE.

LEFT BELOW STORAGE IS CRUCIAL TO THE SUCCESS OF A KITCHEN, AND IT CAN MEAN ANYTHING FROM SLEEK FITTED CUPBOARDS TO AN OPEN-SHELVED DRESSER, AS SHOWN HERE. ONE ADVANTAGE OF THE LATTER IS THAT DISPLAYED ITEMS ARE EASY TO FIND.

OPPOSITE A MIXTURE OF SOLID AND OPEN CUPBOARDS IS AN ATTRACTIVE OPTION BECAUSE IT GIVES THE OPPORTUNITY TO HIDE MOST PARAPHERNALIA OUT OF SIGHT WHILE DISPLAYING THE MORE ATTRACTIVE ITEMS – SUCH AS THE BLUE-AND-WHITE CHINA SEEN HERE. FURNITURE AND TEXTILES CAN BE USED TO BREAK UP THE LINES OF THE ROOM.

Surfaces

Walls in kitchens need to be practical, particularly the areas behind sinks and cooker hobs, which should be moisture-resistant and wipeable. Wall tiles are an effective solution, in terms of both function and style. Single colours or patterns formed by mixing complementary colours look stylish. For a more decorative effect use an ornamental border or place patterned tiles to create focal points. Hand-made tiles with uneven surfaces catch the light in an interesting way and appear to change colour as the day progresses.

When designing a pattern of tiles, such as a chequerboard effect, lay the tiles out on the floor or a large table before fixing them to the wall. This will ensure the pattern is correctly placed and is particularly important if the design is to continue around onto another wall. As when choosing paint or wallpaper, always take a sample of a tile and look at it in the kitchen, not just to check the colour but to consider the tile in relation to the work surfaces it will butt up against.

Tongue-and-groove panelling is another practical solution and adds a more relaxed feel to a kitchen than tiling. It should be painted with a durable, wipeable paint.

Materials for worktops must be suitable from a practical and an aesthetic point of view. Stainless steel looks smart but is high maintenance. Wooden worktops, such as beech, will need coatings of tung oil to protect them from water staining. In a busy family kitchen, which needs to be tough and easy to maintain, it is wise to opt for tried and tested surfaces such as enamel or laminates.

Furniture and storage

Furniture plays a vital role in determining the style and atmosphere of a kitchen. Free-standing pieces, such as a larder cupboard or dresser, create a more casual, relaxed look than sleek fitted units. Plain or painted wooden cupboards suit an informal look, whereas aluminium or black laminate finishes are appropriate for a more graphic style.

A kitchen table should suit the size and shape of the space available. Think about how many people will eat there on a regular basis and decide whether it makes sense to buy the largest table that will fit the space or to opt for a smaller or extendable table in order to accommodate a cupboard for additional storage.

A kitchen that is used for entertaining requires comfortable, upholstered chairs. However, if you have young children, it makes more sense to choose something washable. A sensible compromise is to buy the practical chairs but have loose covers made that can be pulled over them when you want to entertain.

Storage is an essential consideration, not just in terms of the cooking area but for every part of the kitchen. List the items that need to be stored, such as ingredients, cooking tools, crockery, cutlery and table linen. Next consider how much of the storage should be open or concealed; free-standing or fitted. Also assess the role of each piece within the overall design. A dresser or open shelving unit, for example, can be made into a focal point of the kitchen.

Accessibility is vital. Make sure the cupboard doors can be opened as fully as possible and store the ingredients and equipment you use most often within easy reach.

Storage containers are essential for holding ingredients and cooking tools, and they can also add a decorative element to a room, such as glass jars filled with preserved fruit or different kinds of dried pasta.

Lighting

Of all the rooms in the house, the kitchen demands the most care when deciding on a lighting scheme. This is because areas for preparing and cooking food must be adequately and safely lit with spotlights or other task lighting (see page 16). Once you have worked out where units, equipment and furniture are to be positioned, ensure enough lighting is directed towards each area. The other functions of the kitchen will also have an

OPPOSITE IF SPACE ALLOWS, IT IS WORTH DESIGNING THE KITCHEN TO INCLUDE AN EATING AREA, PARTICULARLY IF MEALS ARE NOT EATEN AT THE SAME TIME IN YOUR HOUSEHOLD. A BREAKFAST BAR SUCH AS THIS ONE IS IDEAL FOR QUICK, LIGHT MEALS OR FOR READING THE MORNING PAPER WITH A CUP OF COFFEE.

influence on lighting. The lighting should give you the flexibility to have dimmed lights for intimate suppers or bright lights for reading. As it is such an important room, lighting must be designed both to provide evening illumination and to boost dull days if necessary.

And finally...

If you have inherited a kitchen that works well from a practical point of view, but which is not to your aesthetic taste, consider giving it a quick facelift by changing or painting the unit doors and adding new handles. This can make a remarkable difference, particularly if you also buy new storage containers or rearrange free-standing furniture.

ABOVE LEFT CHOOSE FURNITURE THAT SUITS THE STYLE OF THE KITCHEN. HERE PAINTED CUPBOARDS AND A SOLID WOOD WORKTOP ARE COMPLEMENTED BY TRADITIONALLY SHAPED WOODEN CHAIRS WITH TIE-ON CUSHIONS.

ABOVE RIGHT IN THIS STREAMLINED KITCHEN, INSTEAD OF ACCOMMODATING A RUN OF CUPBOARDS, THE SPACE UNDER THE SINK HAS BEEN TURNED INTO AN ALCOVE FOR THE BIN AND VEGETABLE BOX.

THE SUNNY ASPECT OF THIS
COOL BLUE ROOM HAS BEEN
EXPLOITED TO THE FULL
WITH SHEER CURTAINS AND
A SEMI-SOLID DOOR. IT
CREATES THE PERFECT
AMBIENCE FOR INTIMATE
LUNCH PARTIES AND SHOWS
HOW LITTLE DECORATION IS
NECESSARY TO ACHIEVE AN
ELEGANT EFFECT. THE SEAT
CUSHIONS, IN CONTRASTING
PATTERNS, ADD JUST THE
RIGHT AMOUNT OF WARMTH.

Eating

Eating is one of life's great pleasures. How food is served and the surroundings in which it is eaten are a crucial part of that enjoyment.

Dining areas

Begin by assessing how much dining space you need. Many people find they use the kitchen for every meal from breakfast through to supper, only using the dining room for special occasions and dinner parties. The important points to determine are how many people will be eating together on a day-to-day basis, how many extra people you wish to cater for when the occasion arises, and whether you want to divide where you eat between the kitchen and a dedicated dining room.

If the kitchen is to be used for dining at all times, look for ways of separating the cooking area from the eating one. A simple solution is to use a portable screen made of fabric or painted wood. However, the division does not have to be a physical one. Lighting is an excellent way of defining different parts of a room. You could use a track of bright spotlights for cooking and a downlighter to throw mood lighting onto the dining table. Fit the spotlights with a dimmer switch so they can be turned down while you are eating. Flooring too can be used to separate one part of a room from another, for instance by using wood or tiles for the cooking area and a natural floor covering, such as sisal, in the dining area.

A separate dining room can be totally dedicated to the enjoyment of eating and entertaining. It also offers somewhere to store everything from serving dishes and decanters to cutlery and vases. When deciding on a decorative scheme, think about how the room will look by day and by night. A dining room should be relaxed and welcoming for you and your visitors so choose furniture, fabrics, lighting and details to create this atmosphere.

Furniture and storage

The table is the natural focal point of any dining area. Choose a size and shape of table that suits the proportions of the room, allowing enough space for chairs to be pushed back from it, and for people to move around it. Round tables are generally thought to be more sociable than rectangular ones because they allow people to interact more easily. However, if you need a large table, a rectangular shape may be easier to accommodate than a round one. Extendable tables offer great flexibility, particularly in a space that is used for other activities.

TOP IN A ROOM WITH A MORE NOCTURNAL FEEL, RICH AUTUMNAL COLOURS COMBINE TO CREATE A SANCTUARY IN WHICH GUESTS CAN RELAX. FABRIC WALLING AND FULLY UPHOLSTERED CHAIRS ACCENTUATE THE TEXTURAL ELEMENT OF THE ROOM, WHILE CANDLELIGHT ADDS ATMOSPHERE.

BOTTOM THINK ABOUT HOW THE DINING TABLE LOOKS WHEN NOT IN USE, PARTICULARLY IF IT CAN BE GLIMPSED FROM AN ADJOINING ROOM. IT SHOULD BE CALM AND ORDERED RATHER THAN PILED HIGH WITH CLUTTER. HAVING ONE BIG CENTREPIECE, SUCH AS THIS BASKET OF FLOWERS, GIVES IT A FEELING OF VITALITY. TIE-ON CUSHIONS MAKE A PLEASING VISUAL LINK BETWEEN THE GREENERY ON THE TABLE AND THE CHEQUERED FLOOR.

TOP AND BOTTOM IF YOU LOVE EATING AL FRESCO, MAKE THE
GARDEN AN EXTENSION OF YOUR HOME BY CONTINUING
COLOURS AND PATTERNS FROM THE INTERIOR TO THE TABLE. THE
PAIR OF POTTED BAY TREES HELPS TO SOFTEN THE BOUNDARY
BETWEEN HOUSE AND GARDEN.

RIGHT AN OUTDOOR DINING ROOM CAN LOOK STYLISH TOO –
NOTE PARTICULARLY THE RED STRIPED TOP CLOTH PLACED
OVER THE WHITE ONE. A BIG BUNCH OF SUNFLOWERS ADDS A
DRAMATIC FLOURISH TO THE HEAVILY LADEN TABLE.

A table with an attractive surface, such as smooth
polished or textured wood, will be a feature of the room.
It can be covered with a tablecloth when necessary or you
could use place mats and show it off while dining. If you
buy an antique table, don't feel you must also buy antique
chairs to match. Using traditional and modern pieces
together creates a striking juxtaposition. Even if you
would like a period look in the dining room, it is worth
considering a set of good-quality reproduction dining
chairs. Antique sets can be difficult to source, especially if

you need a large number. Buying pairs of antique chairs is
another option, and will add interest to a room. Finally,
you could purchase one antique chair and have it copied,
although this can be expensive.

Whatever style you choose, make sure chairs
are comfortable; provide seat cushions if they are not
upholstered. Ensure chairs are the correct height for the
table and that they allow plenty of knee room. Position
table and chairs to make the most of natural light. Advice
on dressing a dining table is given on pages 88–91.

Storage furniture includes dressers and cabinets,
although any item in which you can keep plates, cutlery,
glasses and table linen is suitable, as are open shelves. A
side table provides a useful surface on which to carve

meat or assemble dishes. Having somewhere to put salads, fruits, cheeses and wines means you will spend less time running between kitchen and dining table.

Lighting

Well-considered lighting is essential. It should be bright enough for people to see what is on their plates yet subdued enough to create a relaxing atmosphere. Candles bring magic to a room so use as many as possible on the table and elsewhere.

TOP AND BOTTOM FOR A SPECIAL OCCASION, PAY PARTICULAR ATTENTION TO FINISHING TOUCHES. HERE HOME-MADE BUNTING MADE OUT OF FABRIC SCRAPS CREATES A WONDERFUL AMBIENCE AND PICKS OUT THE PINKS AND GREENS OF THE TABLE.

Dining outdoors

A garden makes a wonderful backdrop for meals with family or friends. There may be one area that is used most often, such as a terrace with a built-in barbecue, but it is also enjoyable to make use of different areas in a garden according to the time of day, the occasion and the number of people you wish to seat. A pair of foldaway trestle tables and a portable barbecue will offer you flexibility.

One of the most enjoyable aspects of entertaining outside is making the table look wonderful. You can treat it in two ways: creating a more formal look with large white linen or cotton cloths, good china and crystal glasses, or taking the relaxed route with pretty, patterned linen, an eclectic mix of china and coloured glasses.

LEFT LIGHTWEIGHT, PORTABLE GARDEN FURNITURE ALLOWS YOU TO MOVE YOUR OUTDOOR DINING ROOM TO MAKE THE MOST OF LATE AFTERNOON SUN IN ONE CORNER OF THE GARDEN OR A STUNNING VIEW IN ANOTHER.

Sleeping

Like modern kitchens, bedrooms today have acquired many new roles alongside their traditional ones. As well as being a place to sleep and dress, a bedroom is frequently also somewhere to watch television, listen to the radio, eat breakfast, read a book or write letters. In households with children, the main bedroom is often an important centre for family life. As they are such havens of warmth, comfort and privacy, it is only natural that we should want to use our bedrooms for much more than sleeping.

Beds

Because a good night's sleep is so crucial to our mental and physical well-being, a bed is one of the most important pieces of furniture in a home. Comfort is key so buy the best mattress you can afford and visit a good store so you can test as many as possible. The choice is usually between a mattress that is soft or one that is slightly firm. However, nowadays it is also possible to buy double mattresses that are soft on one half and firmer on the other to suit different requirements.

It makes sense to buy the largest size of bed that is practical for the space. This will imprint a feeling of luxury onto the room and provide plenty of room for movement during sleep. If you have children, you will be grateful for the extra space when they climb into bed with you. When choosing a child's own bed, remember that it should be just as comfortable as one you choose for yourself. Children often want friends to sleep over so use bunk beds or a single bed that has an extra pull-out bed in the base.

Take time to consider the style of bed you would like. A wrought iron, mahogany or antique French bed may appeal but if you are uncertain about style, simplicity is often the best solution. A headboard can be changed and updated relatively easily. As with any major item of furniture, try to imagine the bed in a year's time and ensure that you will not tire of it.

Consider the headboard both in relation to the bed and the height of the room. If you are buying a headboard such as a simple cane design it will usually be available in standard sizes. However, if you are having a headboard made you should be able to specify a size that will suit the proportions of the bed and the room. An upholstered headboard is much more comfortable than a wooden or metal design, especially if you like to read or watch television in bed. Always make comfort the priority when looking at styles.

How you dress the bed will depend on how warm or cool you want to be, how much time you have to maintain the chosen look and the kind of scheme you have put together. It is important to create a calm, relaxing mood so use a mix of textured bed linen with wools and quilted throws (see Bedding, pages 92–95). Changing the bedding is one of the easiest ways of transforming a bedroom.

As the bed is usually such a dominant piece of furniture, it often dictates the style of the room. A four-poster bed, for instance, can be either very decorative or extremely simple. Other pieces of furniture in the room should be chosen to complement this style.

Bedroom atmosphere

A bedroom is a place where we want to feel happy both when waking up in the morning and when relaxing at night. It is important to use colours and textures, materials and furnishings that will create the right atmosphere.

Lighting has a strong influence on mood. Good task lighting will be needed for activities such as applying facial products or reading in bed, but soft, calm lighting is important for when you just want to relax. Dimmer switches and lamps are an easy way of changing the ambience within a bedroom. Candles are romantic but should be placed in hurricane lamps or other forms of containers for safety.

ABOVE LEFT BECAUSE BEDROOMS ARE PRIMARILY, ALTHOUGH NOT EXCLUSIVELY, PLACES FOR SLEEPING, IT IS IMPORTANT THAT THEY ARE DESIGNED TO BE CALM, HARMONIOUS ROOMS. HERE NEUTRAL COLOURS AND SOFT FABRICS CREATE A QUIET OASIS CONDUCIVE TO RELAXATION. AN ARMCHAIR IS NOT ONLY A SEAT, BUT AN ADDITIONAL SURFACE FOR CLOTHES.

ABOVE RIGHT HOW YOU DRESS THE BED IS AS IMPORTANT AS HOW YOU SET A TABLE – IT MAKES A ROOM LOOK COMFORTABLE AND WELCOMING. USING SMALLER CUSHIONS ON TOP OF PILLOWS, AS HERE, RAISES THE HEIGHT OF THE BED AND MAKES IT LOOK EVEN MORE INVITING.

BELOW LEFT HEADBOARDS ARE ESSENTIAL FROM BOTH A PRACTICAL AND A VISUAL POINT OF VIEW. NOT ONLY DO THEY GIVE GOOD BACK SUPPORT FOR WHEN YOU SIT UP IN BED, BUT THEY ALSO ADD A FURTHER DECORATIVE ELEMENT TO THE ROOM. LOOSE-COVERED HEADBOARDS, SUCH AS THE ONE SHOWN HERE, ALSO PROVIDE AN OPPORTUNITY TO SUBTLY ALTER THE SCHEME FROM SUMMER TO WINTER.

BELOW RIGHT BECAUSE OF THE INTIMATE NATURE OF THE SPACE, THE BEDROOM SHOULD BE ONE PLACE WHERE YOU SURROUND YOURSELF WITH LUXURIES AND TREASURES – THINGS THAT LIFT YOUR SPIRITS WHEN YOU WAKE UP IN THE MORNING. EVEN THE SIMPLEST ARRANGEMENT OF FLOWERS, PARTICULARLY SCENTED VARIETIES, CAN MAKE ALL THE DIFFERENCE TO THE AMBIENCE OF A BEDROOM.

The window treatment will also have an impact on mood. It is usually necessary to find a solution that not only suits the style of the room, but will offer the flexibility to allow light in, keep draughts out, and provide privacy. All of these aims can be achieved by using combinations of blinds, voiles, curtains or shutters (see Curtains and Blinds, pages 70–77).

A fireplace in a bedroom can be a real asset. An open fire or a realistic gas fire is wonderfully atmospheric on a winter's evening.

Furniture and storage

Once you have assessed how you would like to use your own bedroom, list the pieces of furniture you will need apart from the bed itself. Bedside tables, chests-of-drawers and wardrobes are basic choices, but you need not be restricted to conventional pieces. For example, a painted or plain wooden side table or chair makes a useful surface for a book or a glass of water. If space allows, your list might also include a sofa, an armchair, a desk, or a table for a television.

The layout of a bedroom is extremely important so begin by drawing a floor plan (see pages 14–15). Allow as much space as possible for movement around the bed and make sure wardrobes, cupboards and chests can be accessed and opened easily. With a large bed, there should be enough space to get in and out on both sides.

Good storage is essential. If you have enough space for a dressing room or walk-in closet, then take advantage of it. By storing clothing in an adjacent space, it is possible to create a bedroom that is much more restful and luxurious. It will also give you more hanging and folding space for your clothes than a cupboard or wardrobe

ABOVE WHEN CHOOSING BEDDING, CONSIDER WHETHER YOU WANT TO LEAVE THE UNDERNEATH OF THE BED EXPOSED. IF NOT, A VALANCE IS THE ANSWER. FOR A DECORATED APPROACH, COORDINATE THIS WITH OTHER TEXTILES WITHIN THE ROOM, SUCH AS THE UPHOLSTERY OR CURTAIN FABRIC. HERE THE SCALLOPED EDGE OF THE BEDSPREAD DRAWS ATTENTION TO THE VALANCE BELOW.

ABOVE A BEDSPREAD OFFERS THE OPPORTUNITY TO INTRODUCE BOLD PATTERN INTO THE SCHEME. THE PLAINER THE PILLOWS AND LINEN ARE, THE MORE IMPACT THE TOP COVER HAS. HERE CUSHIONS HAVE BEEN CHOSEN TO ACCENTUATE THE GEOMETRIC DESIGN, WHILE THE TRIM ON THE PILLOWS PICKS OUT THE SAME COLOURS.

BELOW YOU CAN USE AS MANY LAYERS AS YOU LIKE WHEN DRESSING A BED. IN THIS ROMANTIC BEDROOM, BOLSTER CUSHIONS, PILLOWS AND SCATTER CUSHIONS HAVE BEEN TEAMED WITH VALANCE, LINEN, BLANKET AND EIDERDOWN TO CREATE A SUMPTUOUS EFFECT.

allows. If clothes are to be kept in the bedroom, use space efficiently. One way of creating extra space is to divide your clothes into seasons and keep only those items you need for each season in the bedroom. The rest can be carefully packed up and stored until you need them, possibly in a wardrobe in a guest room.

Finally, consider the visual effect of storage furniture. A wardrobe or large cupboard can often have a very 'solid' look. Glass panelled doors with fabric behind the panels or a specialist paint finish will have a softening effect.

Guest rooms

The essential thing to remember about guest bedrooms is that visitors should feel wanted and pampered. So often, spare bedrooms contain furniture or pictures that are out of favour – or worse, old, uncomfortable beds.

Decide whether to buy one or two single beds, a double, or for the most flexibility, a double bed that unzips to make two single beds. A sofa bed is useful in a guest room, but sleeping on one is not pleasant if it feels like a camp bed. A sofa bed should be comfortable both as a sofa and as a bed. Keep the upholstery relatively plain because you need to think about how it will look in a room as a sofa and when it is made up as a bed. A heavily patterned design will make it difficult to coordinate bedlinen. Dress it as you would a normal bed, paying just as much attention to pillows, sheets, duvets and blankets. Position it in the room carefully, allowing space for movement around it once it is opened. Place tables nearby that can double as bedside tables with surfaces for a lamp, glass of water and a book.

Because a guest room is not in everyday use, you may wish to be bolder with colour or pattern than you might elsewhere. However, remember that the room will be used by a variety of people so the decoration should not be too idiosyncratic.

When deciding what to put in a guest bedroom, it helps to make a list of everything you would like to find in one when you visit someone else. This might include a

glass and a bottle of mineral water, books and magazines, fresh flowers, extra blankets, large bath towels, a notebook and pencil, an alarm clock, a hair drier, a toothbrush and toothpaste, and soap and bath oil. Think of ways to make the visit a memorable one, and don't forget practical needs such as an adequate number of clothes hangers.

ABOVE YOU DO NOT NEED A LOT OF SPACE TO CREATE A REALLY INVITING AND COMFORTABLE GUEST AREA. THIS EXAMPLE HAS BEEN DESIGNED ALONG THE SAME LINES AS A CABIN BED, WITH CUPBOARDS UNDERNEATH FOR LUGGAGE AND SHOES, AND SHELVES ABOVE FOR BOOKS AND GLASSES. AN INFORMAL ARRANGEMENT OF CUSHIONS AND THROWS COMPLETES THE COSY ATMOSPHERE.

OPPOSITE IN THIS GUEST ROOM COLOURS ARE QUIET AND HARMONIOUS, BUT PATTERN HAS BEEN USED TO INTRODUCE CHARACTER AND WARMTH. CHECKS, FLORALS, STRIPES AND PLAINS HAVE BEEN CLEVERLY BLENDED TO CREATE A REALLY WELL THOUGHT OUT SCHEME. THE SIMPLE FOLD-UP CHAIR ALSO DOUBLES AS A SMALL TABLE FOR BOOKS.

Children's Rooms

The important thing to bear in mind for children's rooms is that children do not remain small for very long. This means that any decorative scheme should be able to evolve with time. Before long a pretty nursery will need to develop into a room that is suitable for an active toddler. Storage that was once at adult height must give way to low, open shelves where books and toys can be kept. Just as toddlers have very different needs to babies, so do young children compared with toddlers – and so on through the years.

When deciding on a decorative scheme, remember also that it is not your room. Take your child's opinions and tastes into account and be prepared to compromise a little. If you want your child to enjoy being in the room – and to keep it tidy – it is essential that it reflects his or her interests and personality. Look through books and magazines together to get ideas, and take your child on shopping trips for paints and fabrics. He or she would probably have great fun helping to create an inspiration board (see pages 20–21).

Decoration

Given the need for a room that will evolve with time, it is advisable to use paint on the walls or a colourful textured wallpaper, which could have a vinyl coating for practicality. Choose a cheerful colour that can be used as the backdrop for posters, photographs and other treasured mementos. Specialist blackboard paint can be applied to part of the wall to allow for artistic expression.

Flooring must be practical as well as comfortable. Wooden floors are tough and easy to clean. They can be painted with decorative patterns or chequerboard designs to add interest. Carpet is a more comfortable option, but make sure you choose one that is hard-wearing – a mixture of 80% wool and 20% nylon for strength is a good combination. Opt for a shade that will not show marks too easily. Whatever type of floor you choose, throw big washable rugs over it to introduce colour, pattern, warmth and practicality.

Furnishings – which include not just curtains and upholstery, but bed linen, lampshades and cushions – are a perfect way of changing the look of a child's room easily. Think of how to dress the bed imaginatively, using coloured blankets and throws to enhance the effect. As your child grows older, friends will arrive to stay for the night so be prepared by keeping a futon rolled up in a cupboard, with a spare duvet.

THIS PAGE AND OPPOSITE CHILDREN'S ROOMS PROVIDE A WONDERFUL EXCUSE TO LET THE IMAGINATION RUN RIOT AND DESIGN A SCHEME AROUND A FAVOURITE CHARACTER, HOBBY OR LOCATION. THIS BEDROOM IS SITUATED IN A SEASIDE HOME, SO A NAUTICAL THEME WAS A NATURAL CHOICE. NOT ONLY DID IT INSPIRE THE SHIP-SHAPE BUNK BEDS AND BLUE-AND-WHITE COLOUR SCHEME, BUT IT ALSO SUGGESTED THE TONGUE-AND-GROOVE CUPBOARDS AND SIMPLE CHECKED FABRICS. ACCESSORIES SUCH AS THE LIFE BUOY ON THE BED FRAME AND THE LIGHTHOUSE NIGHT LIGHT FINISH OFF THE LOOK.

Furniture

Child-sized furniture is useful for toddlers and younger children, but it has a limited lifespan. When they are tall enough to use them easily and safely, it is better to give children full-size chairs, desks, chests and wardrobes, and think of ways of customizing them. Decorative paints and stencils are an ideal way of doing this.

There are plenty of novelty beds for children on the market, but again these have a limited lifespan. It makes more sense to buy a conventional design and then use fabrics to add individuality. A good-quality bed with a comfortable mattress is just as essential for a child as it is for an adult. It will also help to ensure a peaceful night's sleep for all.

Bunk beds are useful if space is limited, or for when friends come to stay. Safety is paramount here. When choosing a bunk bed, make sure that it is solidly built, with easy access in and out of both bunks, especially the top one, and that the safety rail on the top bunk does not have a space that is large enough for a child to slip through and then get his or her head stuck.

Another space-saving option is a raised bed with a desk, drawers and cupboard underneath. These can, however, be difficult to move around when cleaning.

When choosing bedroom furniture for an older child, consider what your child uses the room for. Activities may include playing, socializing with friends, hobbies, homework and reading. Think about the furniture needed for these and whether space must be found for computers, televisions, hi-fi systems or other equipment.

Because such a variety of activities take place in a child's room, storage is a key consideration. Depending on the age of the child, space will be needed to store a wide range of items, from toys, games and books to clothes, CDs and sports equipment. You will probably need to use every centimetre of storage space, so as well as installing wardrobes, cupboards, and toy chests, attach pegs to the walls and buy a good supply of wooden or plastic boxes that can be stowed on shelves or under a bed. Books should be easily accessible: while older children can cope with books kept on shelves, a younger child will find it easier to take books from a basket on the floor.

As with anything in a child's room, storage should be safe. Make sure heavy wooden toy chests have safety catches on the lids to prevent injuries to fingers, and that shelves are fixed securely to the wall.

More seems to go into children's rooms than out of them, so regularly extract toys and books that have fallen out of favour or that have been outgrown.

Lighting and accessories

Lighting in a child's room is extremely important. Make sure you provide an overhead light for play, directional light, such as spotlights or an adjustable desk lamp, for reading, writing or drawing, and a soft night light beside the bed for reassurance.

Choose decorative accessories, such as mobiles, pictures and a clock, that are in keeping with the style of the room and the personality of your child. An older child could be given a small budget and allowed to choose his or her own accessories.

THIS PAGE AND OPPOSITE AS MOST PARENTS SECRETLY ADMIT TO THEMSELVES, DECORATING A CHILD'S BEDROOM IS AN EXCUSE TO DESIGN THE ROOM THAT THEY LONGED FOR THEMSELVES AS A CHILD. THIS ROMANTIC SCHEME IS UNASHAMEDLY NOSTALGIC WITH ITS ANTIQUE BEDSTEAD, PATCHWORK-STYLE BEDSPREAD AND RIBBON-EDGED CUSHIONS – ATTENTION TO DECORATIVE DETAIL THAT SHOULD PLEASE EVEN THE MOST STYLE-CONSCIOUS BEAR! IT IS ALSO VERY PRACTICAL: THE BEDS ARE FULL SIZE SO THEY WILL NOT QUICKLY BE OUTGROWN, AND THERE ARE TWO SO THAT FRIENDS CAN COME AND STAY. WOODEN BOARDS, WITH RUGS FOR SOFTNESS, ARE AN IDEAL CHOICE FOR A ROOM THAT NEEDS TO BE PRACTICAL AS WELL AS PRETTY.

Bathing

After the kitchen, the bathroom needs more careful planning than any other room. Bath, shower, sink and lavatory are fixed in place and any mistakes are expensive to rectify. Pipes and wiring are concealed, often by tiling, so it is vital that they guarantee efficiency for many years. Bathrooms must work on two levels: as efficient spaces that you dash into each morning, and as relaxing rooms into which you can retreat in the evening. As well as ensuring that it functions well, it is important to make a bathroom a comfortable place.

Surfaces

Because of the steamy atmosphere and the inevitable water spills and splashes, practicality plays a key role in the choice of surfaces for bathrooms. Ceramic or stone floor tiles are durable, easy to clean and resistant to steam. Softer and warmer alternatives include cork, vinyl and rubber. Carpets can be luxurious but are not practical. Natural floor coverings, such as seagrass, coir and jute, are ideal for a relaxed, simple look.

Ceramic tiles are a practical treatment for walls. Dark-coloured tiles are dramatic but show up marks left by drying water. A functional and elegant alternative is tongue-and-groove panelling. It should be painted with an oil-based paint, which is water-resistant. There is nothing to prevent you from having simple painted walls in your bathroom, provided you again use an oil-based paint, such as eggshell.

Fittings

The style of fittings comes down to personal preference. If you are unsure about colours, white is a classic choice because it is clean and elegant and will go with any other colour. Buy the largest fittings you can for the available space. A large bath is luxurious, while a spacious shower enclosure is a pleasure to use. The shower itself should offer you total control of temperature and water pressure. As with everything else, buy the best you can afford.

The bathroom layout must be designed so the bath, lavatory and any other fittings can be used safely and comfortably. Taking a bath will not be a soothing experience if you feel hemmed in by a sink that is placed too close. Draw a room plan to ensure the most efficient use of the space (see pages 14–15) but bear in mind that it will be very costly to reposition the lavatory because this will mean rerouting the waste pipe. This does, however, give you a starting point for the design.

If space allows, consider positioning the bath centrally in the room to turn it into a focal point and to free-up wall space for an item of storage or to open up a fireplace, if you have one. In a small en-suite bathroom, it may be worth doing without a bath in favour of a generous-sized shower.

LEFT PAYING ATTENTION TO DETAILING IN A BATHROOM WILL MAKE YOUR TIME IN THERE ALL THE MORE ENJOYABLE. THIS SIMPLE WOODEN CHAIR HAS BEEN CLEVERLY PAINTED TO COMPLEMENT THE BLUE-AND-WHITE SCHEME.

Storage and furniture

Storage is needed to accommodate such items as towels, cosmetics, medicines and toiletries. A mixture of hooks, cupboards, open shelves and free-standing units will give you the most options. Try to find space for other pieces of furniture too. A chair is somewhere to put clothes as well as a place to sit. Towelling-covered chairs are cosy and soft, while loose covers in any material are best in terms of practicality.

Lighting and accessories

Lighting should be layered so that it is possible to have a bright light for activities such as shaving or applying make-up and soft light when you want to relax in the bath. Only use lampshades intended for bathrooms; usually made of glass, they fit flush against walls or ceilings, for safety.

Add finishing touches that emphasize comfort and luxury, such as huge towels, towelling robes, scented soaps, fresh flowers and bottles filled with beauty treatments.

CUSTOMIZE TOWELS BY EDGING THEM WITH FABRIC THAT COORDINATES WITH THE REST OF THE BATHROOM SCHEME, SUCH AS THE BLUE-AND-RED GINGHAM HERE. HOME-SEWN FISH IN MATCHING COLOURS ARE A WITTY DETAIL.

THE BATH IS THE FOCAL POINT OF THE BATHROOM, SO CHOOSE ONE THAT SETS THE TONE FOR THE REST OF THE SCHEME. THIS OLD-FASHIONED ROLL-TOP BATH, WITH ORNATE IRON LEGS, IS HANDSOME ENOUGH TO TAKE CENTRE STAGE.

SOFT TEXTURES ARE IMPORTANT IN BATHROOMS BECAUSE THEY SOFTEN THE HARD EDGES OF FIXTURES AND FITTINGS. THE RED LAMPSHADES ON THE MIRROR HERE ARE AN EFFECTIVE TOUCH IN AN OTHERWISE COOL ROOM.

HOOKS ARE IDEAL FOR ANYTHING FROM DRESSING GOWNS AND TOWELS TO FACE FLANNELS AND BAGS. POSITION THEM CAREFULLY SO THEY AND THE ITEMS YOU HANG ON THEM DO NOT GET IN YOUR WAY.

FABRIC BAGS ADD A NOTE OF SOFTNESS TO A BATHROOM AND ARE USEFUL FOR STORING SMALL ITEMS LIKE SOAP AND TOOTHPASTE. MAKE SEVERAL FOR STORING DIFFERENT ITEMS.

PEGBOARDS ARE USEFUL FOR STORING SEVERAL TOWELS AND FLANNELS. YOU CAN HANG THEM HIGH UP AROUND THE ROOM, SHAKER-STYLE, OR LOWER DOWN, AS ON THIS PANELLED WALL.

Outside

Outside areas such as terraces, roof gardens and courtyards are valuable extensions to a home. The colour and scent of plants, the sound of birdsong and the open sky all combine to create a wonderful atmosphere for relaxing or for socializing with friends. Food always tastes better outdoors, and a well designed and furnished outside room will transform the simplest of meals into a memorable occasion.

Furniture

Seating and tables can be built-in features although portable furniture will give you more flexibility. Outdoor chairs in aluminium or treated timber offer year-round durability, but provided you have the storage space to protect them from rain or frost, any type of chair can be used, or you can simply bring indoor chairs outside. Cane or painted wooden chairs are popular for a relaxed look, while lightweight folding canvas chairs are stylish and easy to move around and stow. Deckchairs offer colour and character but they are not practical for eating. Use cushions to soften hard seating, both visually and for comfort.

Choose a size and shape of table that will seat you and your family or friends, and that will fit the space most comfortably, allowing enough room for chairs to be pulled back and for people to move around. For bigger gatherings, use a trestle table (see pages 142–143).

Tents and canopies provide style, shade and shelter. Being shower-proof, they can be a full-time feature of an outdoor room from spring to autumn. Add wicker chairs, throws and cushions to give them a lived-in feel.

Lighting

Lighting extends the time you can spend outside and creates a magical atmosphere for outdoor dining. Even very simple lighting can have enormous impact: strands of white outdoor fairy lights can be trailed over a trellis or a pergola, while hurricane lamps for candles or night lights for the table bring romance to an evening meal. Scented candles will also deter insects.

Cooking

When dining outside you could simply serve up cooked meals or salads prepared in your kitchen. However, a barbecue adds fun and flavour to outdoor entertaining. A brick barbecue should be built in a safe and sheltered spot in the garden. A gas barbecue will allow al fresco cooking for a much greater part of the year. Portable barbecues can be trundled around the garden to catch the sun or avoid the wind.

Plants and accessories

There is an enormous range of plants to choose from, depending on the effect you want to create. Choose climbing roses and clematis for a romantic look; clipped box and standard bays for classic formality, or architectural phormiums, grasses and bamboos for a modern feel.

Scent is important, especially for enhancing the mood at night, so grow climbers such as jasmines and honeysuckles on trellis and aromatic herbs such as lavender and rosemary in containers. In warmer regions it might be possible to grow Mediterranean species such as bougainvilleas.

If you have doors leading from the house onto a terrace or courtyard, emphasize the link between indoors and out by using the same containerized plants each side of the door.

Choose containers that complement the colour, form and texture of the plants, but also think about the overall style of the space. A smart Versailles box has quite a different feel to a recycled enamel bucket or a simple terracotta pot.

Accessories are just as important in outdoor rooms as they are indoors. Old garden tools or watering cans are atmospheric; baskets of harvested fruit and vegetables or bunches of drying herbs add seasonal interest; or you could simply display objects found in the garden or nearby, such as shapely stones or shells, fragments of china or weathered pieces of wood. Such items can be changed regularly so there is always something new to enjoy.

THIS PAGE AND OPPOSITE
WHEN DECORATING AN OUTSIDE
ROOM, THINK ABOUT HOW YOU
CAN BORROW ELEMENTS FROM
INSIDE THE HOUSE TO CREATE
A FEELING OF CONTINUITY.
CUSHIONS SOFTEN THE LINES OF
HARD FURNITURE AND BRING
PATCHES OF CONTRASTING
COLOUR INTO THE LANDSCAPE.
ACCESSORIES CAN ALSO BE USED
TO LINK INDOORS AND OUT.

REVITALIZATIONS

TIMELY CHANGES

A home may be enclosed by walls but this does not mean it cannot embrace the world outside.

The importance of assessing natural light when choosing colours, and of considering the view from windows when selecting curtains and blinds, was discussed earlier in the book. Once you recognize the influence of the external environment on your home, it is satisfying to take this a step further and think of ways to reflect the seasons in the decorative scheme. For example, if you have a garden or a country view, you could take inspiration from the succession of colours in flowers and foliage. And even if you do not, the changes that occur to light, temperature and weather as the seasons progress create distinct moods that can be echoed in an interior scheme. In urban settings this is an important way of retaining a link with nature.

Seasonal decorating is neither difficult nor time-consuming. It is a question of ensuring that all the main ingredients of a scheme – the walls, floors and major pieces of furniture – complement each other and create a solid foundation, while using accessories to change the look. For example, you could use warm wool plaid cushions in winter and crisp linen and cotton ones in summer. Plants and flowers are an obvious way of reflecting the seasons – think of vases filled with vibrant yellow daffodils in spring, and large bowls of holly stems in winter.

On a different time-scale, the transition from day to night can also be reflected in an interior scheme, in order to transform the function and mood of a space.

Another type of timely change is to give a room an entirely new look for a celebration. Styling an interior for a special day or evening will make the occasion a memorable one.

Winter into Summer

The passing of the seasons not only heralds a change in temperature, but also affects the quality of light, which in turn is responsible for the way we feel both physically and emotionally. Winter makes us long for a cosier, safer, more insular environment. When summer dawns, our instinct is to open the windows and let the world back in.

Reflecting these changing moods in our homes is both evocative and invigorating. It also enhances the level of comfort. A room that has a heavy, oppressive atmosphere on a hot summer's day is as unwelcoming as one that is bare and draughty on a cold day in

winter. Unless you have a suite of rooms for winter or summer living, each room you design should acknowledge the changing seasons.

The secret is to think of the structure of the room – walls, floor and ceiling – as a blank canvas onto which different moods can be painted. If you keep these large expanses relatively neutral, it is then possible to introduce layers of mood through textiles, windows treatments, lighting and accessories. The key point is that if a room is going to be in constant use all year round, it is best to avoid very rich, wintry colours or summery pastel ones for the main items such as sofas, chairs and curtains. This also applies to pattern designs – avoid using patterns with

LEFT AND FAR LEFT BY CHOOSING NEUTRAL-COLOURED UPHOLSTERY FABRIC, IT BECOMES EASY TO RING THE CHANGES WITH THROWS AND CUSHIONS. HERE AQUAMARINE AND BLUE CREATE A COOL SEASIDE LOOK WHICH REFLECTS THE COLOURS AND TEXTURES OF THE COASTAL LANDSCAPE OUTSIDE. THESE SHADES HAVE BEEN REPEATED THROUGHOUT THIS LIVING ROOM, AND ARE COMPLEMENTED BY A TREASURED COLLECTION OF LOCAL POTTERY.

BELOW IN WINTER, THE
LOOSE COVERS SHOWN
LEFT ARE REMOVED AND
REPLACED BY WARM
PLAID SEAT CUSHIONS.
THE WOOL RUG AND
RICHLY COLOURED
TABLECLOTH ALSO HELP
TO MAKE THE ROOM
FEEL COSY.

strong seasonal colour connotations. Textures
too should not be so heavy nor so light
that they only work well at certain times
of the year. If you are decorating in winter,
try to imagine how the colours and fabrics
would look in the heat of the summer.
Reverse the process if you are designing the
room in summer.

Once you have achieved a look that
will work well whatever the month, the
simplest way to change its atmosphere is to
alter the accessories. Lamps, for example, are
a necessity in winter, even during the day.
However, they might be positioned differently

in summer, when they are used only at night.
Keep lamp bases the same, but use different
shades in darker or lighter colours according
to the time of year.

Decorative objects, pictures, photo
frames or vases can also be used to ring the
seasonal changes. It may seem extravagant to
buy things that are on display for only a few
months each year, but it is far easier to
change the accessories in a room than the
major elements. Unpacking items that have
been stored away also allows you to see
them anew and to move them into different
positions. Rooms that are static can become
dull, so this rotation of winter and summer
looks helps to maintain vitality.

RIGHT AND FAR RIGHT
AS AUTUMN PROGRESSES,
THE SOFA IN THE ROOM
SEEN LEFT IS MOVED
FROM ITS POSITION
FACING THE WINDOW TO
FACE INWARD TOWARDS
THE FIRE. CUSHIONS
AND THROWS ARE
EXCHANGED FOR ONES
IN DEEP, EARTH TONES
OF TERRACOTTA, RED,
OCHRE AND BROWN,
WHILE THE WALL-
HANGING REFLECTS THE
CHANGE OF MOOD. THE
ITEMS ON THE SHELVES
ARE CHANGED FOR ONES
THAT COMPLEMENT THIS
MORE ROBUST LOOK.

Flowers too should be in keeping with the time of year. In fact, choosing flowers should be like seasonal cooking. As with food, buying flowers seasonally is also cheaper. On an aesthetic level, it is a way of relating your home to what is happening in nature. In winter, think of holly with berries and exotic touches such as white orchids. In spring, there is nothing better to lift the spirits than bowls of hyacinths or velvety anenomes. Summer is epitomized by the romance of *Alchemilla mollis* and cabbage roses – and anything you can cut from your own garden. Autumn arrangements should have rich tones such as reds and russets, which could be reflected in flowers and foliage.

ABOVE AND TOP COLOUR AND TEXTURE ARE PIVOTAL WHEN CHANGING A ROOM FOR THE SEASONS. IN THIS LIVING ROOM, THE LEATHER ARMCHAIR, RED PAISLEY THROW ON THE SOFA AND GENEROUS SPICE-COLOURED CUSHIONS ALL PLAY THEIR PART IN CREATING AN ATMOSPHERE OF WARMTH AND COSINESS. THE RED VELVET CURTAINS, BASKET OF LOGS AND JUTE MAT EMPHASIZE THE FEELING OF PROTECTION AGAINST THE CHILL OF WINTER.

Scent is also important. A room should be imbued with the scent of the season, be it sweet peas in summer or cut pine at Christmas. Think laterally: herbs such as sprigs of rosemary smell wonderful in summer, and fruits and spices such as oranges and cinnamon are redolent of winter.

Floors too offer seasonal flexibility. If you lay a hard floor first you can add richly patterned rugs and runners for the winter months, but remove them in warm weather when it is pleasing to feel something cool underfoot. Natural flooring is also an excellent base, as it too can be dressed for winter or left bare for summer simplicity. If you favour carpet, then choose one in neutral tones and add rugs on top in winter for a warmer, more decorative look.

While the major pieces of furniture, such as sofas and tables, are likely to remain unchanged, it makes sense to use a new set of runners, a tablecloth, throws, loose covers or cushions to make them warmer and cosier for winter, or lighter and airier for summer.

The layout of furniture need not be static. While it is natural in winter to group seating around the fireplace, it is equally natural in summer to rearrange it to give a more open feeling or to take advantage of an outside view. Consider also introducing occasional furniture for the time of year — in a living room, for example, you could swap a wooden coffee table for a glass one, or a leather chair for a painted one.

Window treatments are another important way of transforming a space seasonally. In winter the priority is to keep cold draughts and depressing grey days out. This calls for heavy, lined curtains, perhaps combined with shutters or blinds. In summer there is an urge to allow light and fresh air back into a room — take down the curtains and exchange them for lightweight sheers or let the blinds or shutters suffice on their own.

Once you begin to take the seasons into account, it can add a whole new level of interest to a decorative scheme. Psychologically it can be satisfying too: don't we all long to batten down the hatches in winter and then let our spirits soar in summer?

ABOVE AND TOP THE SAME ROOM HAS BEEN GIVEN A FRESH LOOK FOR SUMMER BY COVERING UPHOLSTERY IN WHITE LOOSE COVERS AND CUSHIONS IN BLUES AND WHITES. THE SIDE TABLE IS NOW COVERED IN A BLUE-AND-WHITE CHECKED CLOTH AND HAS BEEN MOVED TO TAKE THE PLACE OF THE LOG BASKET. THE FURNITURE HAS ALSO BEEN SPACED OUT TO GIVE THE ROOM AN AIRIER FEEL, COMPLEMENTED BY THE BREEZY SHEERS AT THE WINDOW.

RIGHT AND BELOW SOME ROOMS CAN HAVE DIFFERENT FUNCTIONS DEPENDING ON THE TIME OF DAY. THIS INGENIOUS SPACE IS A STUDY BY DAY, WITH A COSY AREA FOR RELAXING, AND A GUEST BEDROOM AT NIGHT. IN SUCH ROOMS IT IS IMPORTANT TO PROVIDE ENOUGH STORAGE TO CATER FOR EACH ROLE. IN THE STUDY AREA HERE, SHELVING HAS BEEN MADE OUT OF UPTURNED ORANGE BOXES.

Day into Night

Altering a room from day to night may be necessary both to effect a change in use and to reflect a change in atmosphere. Such changes can either be significant, as is the case with a room that converts into a guest bedroom, or simple, as with a living room that is used by the whole family during the day, but becomes a peaceful sanctuary for adults in the evening.

A room that converts to a bedroom must be carefully planned at the outset to accommodate each role and to make the transition from one to the other as easy as possible. A sofa bed or day bed will provide both a place to sleep and an additional area for relaxing. Ensure there is space around the bed for freedom of movement. If the sleeping area is in a home office consider erecting a curtain that can be pulled across at night to screen off the working area and create a more restful environment.

A mixture of lighting is needed to cater to the change in use. A table lamp by the bed will enhance the mood and provide a light for reading. Choose suitable task lighting for the other activities that take place in the room.

Family living rooms that need to be reclaimed each evening require plenty of storage for tidying away toys and games in a hurry. Baskets and ottomans are useful, and a decorative chest of drawers is ideal for storing numerous items. A layered lighting scheme, which could include candles or lanterns, will enable you to switch easily between energetic family activities and calm relaxation.

Another area where you may wish to alter the mood from day to night is the dining room or an eating area in a kitchen. Using loose covers on dining chairs, crisp white table linen and plenty of candles is a quick and simple way of enhancing a supper party.

AT NIGHT THE SOFA BED IS SCREENED OFF FROM THE REST OF THE ROOM WITH A CHECKED CURTAIN, WHILE A THICK BLIND HAS BEEN CHOSEN FOR THE WINDOW TO BLOCK OUT MORNING SUNLIGHT. AT NIGHT, THIS MAKES THE SPACE FEEL LIKE A ROOM WITHIN A ROOM. CLEAN BEDDING IS KEPT IN THE BASKET NEXT TO THE BED, WHILE THE ANGLEPOISE LAMP DOUBLES AS READING LIGHT OR BEDSIDE LAMP. THE PEGBOARD AT THE OTHER SIDE OF THE CURTAIN IS A CONVENIENT PLACE FOR GUESTS TO HANG CLOTHES OR WASHBAGS.

Inside to Outside

The external environment is an important and ever-changing influence on a home, and it is satisfying to link the two. When choosing window treatments, for example, as well as considering the decorative scheme inside, make sure they are in sympathy with the views outside. A good view, such as countryside or the sea, can be accentuated with a fabric in similar shades.

If you have a garden, the view is as important from outside to inside as it is the other way around. Again sympathetic window treatments should be used as a frame. Windowboxes are seen from the outside and the inside so plant flowers that echo the colours in both house and garden. Choose cushions and loose covers for garden furniture that complement those in your home – then you can select tableware, glasses and cutlery that work as well outside as they do indoors.

THIS PAGE AND OPPOSITE
IF A ROOM LOOKS ONTO A
BEAUTIFUL GARDEN, DRAW
ATTENTION TO THE VIEW
WITH TRANSLUCENT FABRIC,
SUCH AS THESE VOILE
CURTAINS WITH A BAY TREE
MOTIF. THE TRUG OF GREEN
VEGETABLES ALSO HELPS TO
LINK HOUSE AND GARDEN.
THE GARDEN TABLE HAS BEEN
SET WITH LINEN, GLASSES
AND OTHER ITEMS THAT ARE
IN KEEPING WITH THOSE IN
THE HOUSE.

Seasonal Celebrations

There is one word that should always be linked to the idea of celebration and that is enjoyment. This applies not only to your guests, but to you. It is all too easy to become so exhausted by the organization of an event that we fail to enjoy it ourselves.

The golden rule is to make any celebration as easy as possible and to plan it well in advance. Set yourself a realistic time scale and budget, and

champagne or gifts in velvet bags to hang on the backs of chairs at Christmas – will make an impression on your guests.

If you are expecting more people than you would usually entertain, use extra spaces around your home. If they are large enough, halls can make wonderful settings for special dinners, as can reception rooms from which the main furniture has been cleared. In the

LEFT AND RIGHT
A LARGE HALL IS
AN IDEAL SETTING
FOR A SPECIAL
OCCASION. IN
SUMMER THE MOOD
IS SET BY FLORAL
SEAT COVERS AND A
PRETTY SCALLOPED
TABLECLOTH.

decide on an appropriate theme, such as a colour or an idea relating to the season, that will be relatively easy to carry out.

Do not feel you should make all the decorative elements yourself. Shops are bursting with wonderful accessories for parties so seek out interesting items. You should save enough time to add a few individual touches that will make it seem as if the whole event has been hand-crafted. Even the simplest ideas – such as calligraphic place cards, bags of chocolate coins wrapped in coloured tissue paper for children, strawberries to float in the

summer, a garden lawn or terrace can be ideal for entertaining but never rely on having fine weather – try to have an ancillary plan should the heavens open. Shower-proof garden canopies are a worthwhile investment for this reason.

Do not worry if none of the chairs match or if you have to push two tables together. The art of disguise is key – you can distract attention from any imperfections by creating a splendid table setting. Keep your theme simple but layer it for a bold effect. Finally, do not forget the importance of lighting for an evening party, whether it is indoors or in the garden.

THE SAME HALL IS ALSO USED FOR
CHRISTMAS DINNER, WHEN THE
RICHLY PATTERNED RUG, CHECKED
SEAT CUSHIONS AND MATCHING
UNDERCLOTH TRANSFORM IT
COMPLETELY FROM THE SUMMER
LOOK SEEN LEFT. TRAILS OF IVY AND
SCARLET RIBBON ARE ALL THE
ACCESSORIES NEEDED

A TOUCH OF COLOUR

OPPOSITE YOU CAN
ACHIEVE IMPACT IN A ROOM
BY USING VERY LITTLE
COLOUR, BUT USING IT
BOLDLY. THIS CURTAIN
DRAPE COMBINES
CONFIDENT STRIPES OF
BLUE AND CREAM AGAINST A
YELLOW GINGHAM CHECK.
THE EFFECT IS EXUBERANT
AND SUMMERY, GIVING A
CLEAR MESSAGE ABOUT
THE RELAXED STYLE OF
THE HOME.

ABOVE COBALT BLUE MAKES
A VIVID ACCENT COLOUR
AGAINST CREAM-PAINTED
TONGUE-AND-GROOVE
WALLS. THESE SMALL
PATCHES OF COLOUR ARE
IMPORTANT BECAUSE THEY
SEND OUT VIBRATIONS
THROUGHOUT A ROOM.
EVERY INGREDIENT YOU
INTRODUCE INTO A SCHEME
HAS AN EFFECT IN TERMS OF
COLOUR, EVEN SOMETHING
AS MODEST AS A BAG.

Colour is such a powerful force that even small amounts of it can have dramatic effects. In a neutral room, for example, highlights of red, orange or yellow will completely change the mood from calm and restful to lively and vibrant.

Touches of colour are a way of breathing new life into a scheme without the need to redecorate walls or replace curtains or upholstery. They can take the form of cushions, blankets, vases, lampshades, candles, tableware, glasses, runners, rugs – anything that is easy to change or move. Although often small in size, the impact of such items can be immense, not only in terms of colour, but in bringing cohesion to a room.

As well as using single accent colours it is possible to create wonderful effects with a combination of shades – chocolate brown and powder blue, for example, or mint green with amethyst. You could even mix them on the same object, such as a cushion, then send out echoes through the scheme with items in either colour.

Touches of colour can also be used to soften or subtly change the dominant shade in the room. For instance, combining blue with green creates a rich, dark effect, while adding yellow to green gives a much fresher, lighter look.

Accent colours are perfect for experimenting with strong, atmospheric shades that could be overpowering when used on a wall or a sofa. They also enable you to introduce fashionable colours without having to make a long-term commitment to them.

Using colour in this way will only work well if you are disciplined about your possessions. If there are too many colours vying for attention, the result will be confusion. Edit items carefully, deciding which to keep, which to add, and which would look better in another part of your home. Such discipline can reap rich rewards. As the following pages show, the simplest ideas often have the most impact.

Colour Changes

Colour is one of the quickest and most effective ways of giving a room a facelift. If you want to revitalize your home with colour, the first thing to do is step back and look at the shades of the existing scheme. The eye naturally focuses on the big planes of colour: walls, floors, windows and major pieces of furniture. But look also at the smaller objects such as lamps, vases, cushions and collections of china. The chances are that these have little to link them, for the simple reason that most of us buy such objects because we like them individually rather than thinking how they will fit into a whole scheme. If you want

DECORATIVE DETAILS CANGES BE USED TO ALTER THE COLOUR OF A ROOM WITHOUT NEEDING TO CHANGE THE MAJOR ELEMENTS. HERE CREAMS AND NEUTRAL COLOURS CREATE A CALM, RESTFUL MOOD WITH ELEMENTS INCLUDING IVORY BALLS IN MARBLE URNS ON THE MANTELPIECE, A CREAM-COLOURED CHINA DISH FULL OF BONE-HANDLED CUTLERY ON THE COFFEE TABLE, AND CUSHIONS IN TONES OF OATMEAL, CREAM AND TAUPE ON THE SOFA.

to give a room impact, look for ways of achieving a more cohesive look. Colour is an excellent way of doing this as it can create an illusion of complete redecoration when in fact key components are unchanged. The secret is to use flashes of colour and echo them throughout the scheme.

It is easier to use touches of colour if you can begin with an area decorated in calm, blended tones. It might be a room based around creams or beiges, or perhaps different shades of blue, green or terracotta – what is important is that there should not be too many colours in the basic scheme.

EXCHANGING ONE GROUP OF ACCESSORIES FOR ANOTHER GIVES THE ROOM SHOWN OPPOSITE A FRESH NEW CHARACTER. THE SOFA HAS BEEN DRESSED WITH PATTERNED CUSHIONS IN BLUE AND AMETHYST AND A WOOLLEN BLANKET EDGED WITH RED. AMETHYST GLASSES ON THE COFFEE TABLE AND DECORATIVE ANTIQUE CHINA ON THE MANTELPIECE HAVE BEEN CHOSEN TO HARMONIZE WITH THE COLOURS IN THE ROOM.

Bear this in mind if you are thinking of decorating a room from the beginning.

You can then achieve a colour transformation by choosing one strong accent colour – anything from acid green or strong pink to midnight blue or burnt orange – and introducing this into key pieces within the room. In a living room, that could be cushions, blinds to hang behind curtains, objects and ceramic pieces. In a bedroom, it could include blankets over the bed, fabric-lined baskets for toiletries, lampshades and

changes by having loose covers made in timeless, elegant linen. This will completely alter the look of the room. Similarly, a bed that is dressed in simple white cotton with a white piqué bedspread appears very different to one covered in a soft-coloured chequerboard blanket. As with colours, these textural changes will have more impact in a neutral scheme.

Use touches of colour to make a room unique. For example, you could add a border in the accent colour to the curtains

rugs. In a dining room, it might mean wine glasses, table linen, candles and runners over chairs. When seen against the blank canvas of the room itself, these blocks of bold colour will lift the scheme and create a whole new look.

Once you have chosen the accent colour, look out for other suitable pieces to add. Try to build up enough accessories for both a winter and a summer look.

Changes of fabric are an effective way of revitalizing a colour scheme, as they introduce different textures and so affect atmosphere. For example, if your dining chairs are upholstered in a deep, rich fabric such as a bordeaux-coloured velvet, ring the

or to a plain tablecloth, or use the colour in piping on cushions. You could also apply a coloured wash to picture frames to echo the accent shade.

ABOVE LEFT THESE ANTIQUE SODA SIPHONS WITH FABULOUS BLUE BASES WERE CHOSEN NOT ONLY FOR THEIR INTEREST, BUT BECAUSE THEY HIGHLIGHTED OTHER COLOURS IN THE ROOM. THE APPLES AND LEMONS PROVIDE A VIVID CONTRAST.

ABOVE RIGHT IF YOU WANT TO CREATE A DRAMATIC EFFECT, MATCH FABRICS TO KEY OBJECTS IN THE ROOM. THE CUSHIONS AND CERAMIC POT SHOWN HERE ARE PERFECT COMPANIONS TO THE PAINTING BEHIND.

OPPOSITE WHEN THE ROOM IS SEEN AS A WHOLE, IT IS CLEAR HOW LITTLE HIGHLIGHT COLOUR HAS BEEN USED IN PROPORTION TO THE BASE COLOUR, BUT HOW GREAT ITS IMPACT IS VISUALLY.

STYLE MAKERS

OPPOSITE
OBJECTS THAT HAVE
ACQUIRED A PATINA OF
WEAR AND USE HAVE ADDED
RESONANCE, SUCH AS THIS
RUSTIC-LOOKING PAINTED
WOODEN FRUIT BOWL. THE
WHITE LINEN CLOTH
PROVIDES THE PERFECT
BACKDROP.

BELOW RIGHT
AN OLD ENAMEL WATER JUG
AND A PRETTY PAINTED
MUSHROOM BOX MAKE A
STILL-LIFE IN BLUE AND
WHITE. THE WHITE TONGUE-
AND-GROOVE PANELLING
AND THE PLAIN WOODEN
TABLE ACCENTUATE THE
SIMPLE BEAUTY OF THE
OBJECTS.

Style makers are the crucial elements that can finish a scheme off perfectly. Including anything from handcrafted items and antiques to flowers and found objects, these are the decorative details that are often small in size but big in impact. In design terms, they play a vital role in creating accents of colour, form and texture in a room. Displayed either singly or in groups, they provide a focus for the eye and greatly enrich an interior scheme.

However, these elements are not merely accessories. The objects you collect and the paintings you hang on the walls express your personality and invest your home with a unique character and style. These items are also enjoyable to buy or find, and are frequently discovered by chance in junk shops and antiques fairs.

Unlike flooring materials, furniture or upholstery, decorative details are often not so expensive that they cannot be easily changed should you tire of the look or discover something new. Neither are they as inconvenient to replace as major purchases. When you decide to make changes, pack them up into storage boxes, and you will be delighted to rediscover them in a few months' time. This is important because revitalizing a home does not necessarily mean buying new items. Often it is a question of taking what you have and making more of it. Something as simple as hanging paintings in different locations or changing lampshades will add fresh interest to an interior scheme.

This chapter explains how to use style makers to breathe new life into your home with very little effort.

Decorative Objects

Having the main colour scheme and items of furniture in place should not be the end of the decorating story. If you want a room to have a professional edge, look for ways of picking up themes and echoing them in small details. Using these items effectively provides an opportunity to layer an interior scheme, thereby accentuating the colours, patterns, shapes and textures within the room.

Some accessories are purely decorative, but others, such as candlesticks and vases, have a functional role too. It is important when completing a room to be aware of this difference. Function must determine where something is placed, in terms of both height and location. Decide which of the objects you wish to be prominent and place them at key focal points in the room. Use other objects in a supporting role.

Purely decorative accessories are only worth including if you display them well. Location is important, especially the colour they are set against, how they are lit and whether it is a single object that becomes a focal point or a group that needs to be carefully arranged for maximum effect. It is not dissimilar to creating a still life. The idea is to provide little pockets of interest to please the eye no matter how the room is viewed.

Review accessories every few months to keep your home looking and feeling fresh and interesting. If you want to give a new look to a room, the easiest way to do so without redecorating is to change the more portable items around. Rotate them from room to room and you will enjoy them all the more. Remember that decorating your home is only the beginning: living in it means allowing it to change on a continual basis.

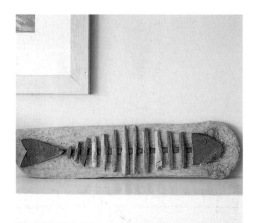

Display

The way objects and pictures are displayed plays a crucial part in the success of a room. Consider pictures first. Do not dot these around a room – one on each wall – as this will only emphasize the spaces between them. Instead group them together on one wall, even if it means leaving the other three bare. If they are pictures of similar subject matter, size and frame, accentuate this connection by making the arrangement symmetrical. A group of six, for example, lends itself to a two-by-three display. Pictures that are double hung, one on top of the other, also look eye-catching, particularly in rooms where they are often viewed from a sitting position such as dining or living rooms. Or you might take a contemporary approach by hanging them in a horizontal line along one wall, or leaning them against the wall or on a mantelpiece.

If you have a group of pictures or other wall-mounted objects that vary in size, shape and style, lay them out on the floor first and move them around until you find a composition that works. Space them carefully and measure the distance between each one, so you can pencil outlines onto the wall where they should be positioned. If you want to ensure that none of them are lop-sided when hung, use two picture hooks side by side as opposed to one.

If you have a magnificent painting or a wonderfully decorative mirror, then it might be strong enough to stand on its own rather than be part of a display. Mirrors can make even the smallest of living rooms take on a sense of importance.

Finally, consider how objects are arranged on surfaces such as tables or mantelpieces. For visual impact, group similar objects together – just as you would with pictures; they then take on the same role as a collection.

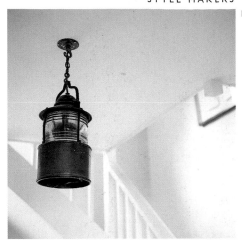

Lighting

Although lighting has already been considered in terms of illumination, it is important to remember that lights and lamps have a decorative role to play too. As with other ingredients within the home, the golden rule is not to impulse buy; apply the same level of consideration to lights as you would to furniture or fabrics. If you want a light that is decorative as well as functional, then decide how big it needs to be for its chosen location and purpose and how it might reflect the style of the room in terms of colour, material and shape. Remember too that, generally speaking, lamps and wall lights work well in pairs.

Table lamps come in a bewildering range of sizes and shapes. Think about the base first: should this be chosen to blend into the main colour scheme or would you prefer one in an accent colour? Should it be plain or patterned, high or low, slim or round? If you can't find a conventional design you like, you may be able to customize one by using a suitable jar, pot or urn – as long as a reputable electrician does the wiring for you. For something more individual, scour antiques shops for old lamp bases.

Lampshades too come in a wide variety of colours, sizes, shapes and styles. Again it is possible to decorate your own by stencilling motifs onto a card shade. If you are not sure which size to buy, measure from the base of the lamp to the bulb socket; that height should be the same as the circumference of the shade.

Central ceiling pendants should never be the only source of lighting within a room – the light can look dull when diffused so much – but they can add another layer of interest, particularly when positioned so they are reflected in a mirror. Remember that the more imposing the design, the more it will pull the eye upwards.

Flowers and Plants

Cut flowers and container plants offer the perfect way of introducing nature into a room. Their vivid colours, bold shapes, textural leaves and delicious scents will all lift a scheme. They also send out a more subliminal message: bringing in fresh arrangements of flowers, be they blooms from the garden or twigs from the hedgerows, shows that you care for your home and the way it looks, feels and smells.

What kind of flowers or plants you choose is an entirely personal decision. The important thing is that the colours should complement those of the room. Living rooms and hallways lend themselves to bold displays of flowers or plants, but in a bedroom you might prefer something less intrusive such as sweet peas. On a decorative side table, you could have one large bowl of planted bulbs. For a modern approach, buy a set of small matching glass vases and place them in a row with a single stem in each one or plant single bulbs in matching containers.

Build up a collection of different shapes and sizes of containers – these should reflect both the flowers you are planning to use and the style and colour of the room itself. Galvanized metal or chunky clear glass is effective in a contemporary setting; blue-and-white or creamware jugs are wonderful in more traditional rooms.

When considering scents, think laterally: a large basket of dried lavender smells delicious as well as bringing colour and texture to a room. Remember that almost anything natural can make an arrangement: for example, a huge bunch of parsley in a round silver pot or a large vase of willow stems with catkins can be eye-catching.

Sources

Retail outlets for interior decoration are many and varied. The following is a selection of Jane Churchill fabric stockists and other suppliers that I would recommend.

JANE CHURCHILL STOCKISTS

Main Showroom

Jane Churchill
151 Sloane Street
London SW1X 9BX
Tel: 020 7730 9847
Also paints, lighting, upholstered furniture, trimmings

Department Stores

Arighi Bianchi
Commercial Road
Macclesfield
Cheshire SK10 1LH
Tel: 01625 613333

Bentalls Plc
Anstee House
Kingston upon Thames KT1 1TX
Tel: 020 8546 1001

Fenwick Ltd
39 Northumberland Street
Newcastle upon Tyne NE99 1AR
Tel: 0191 232 5100

Hoopers
4 Mount Pleasant
Tunbridge Wells
Kent TN1 1QT
Tel: 01892 530222

Insider Dealings
135 Chiswick High Road
London W4 2EA
Tel: 020 8994 1030

Jenners Ltd
48 Princes Street
Edinburgh EH2 2YT
Tel: 0131 225 2442

John Lewis
Oxford Street
London W1A 1EX
Tel: 020 7629 7711
And all John Lewis Partnership stores countrywide

Lee Longlands (Birmingham)
224 Broad Street
Birmingham B15 1AZ
Tel: 0121 6439101

Liberty
Regent Street
London W1R5 LA
Tel: 020 7734 1234

Specialist Decorating Shops

A.F. Drysdale Ltd
35 North West Circus Place
Edinburgh EH3 6TW
Tel: 0131 225 4686

Coleshill Interiors and Antiques
14 High Street
Warwick B46 1AZ
Tel: 01675 467416

Designworks
38 Gibson Street
Glasgow G12 8NX
Tel: 0141 339 9520

Dragons
23 Walton Street
London SW3 2HX
Tel: 020 7589 3795

Jamandic Ltd
22 Bridge Street Row
Chester CH1 1NN
Tel: 01244 312822

James Brindley of Harrogate
29–31 James Street
Harrogate HG1 1QY
Tel: 01423 560757

Margaret Sheridan
36 Market Place
Norwich NR9 4AF
Tel: 01953 850691

Mary Ensor Ltd
37 High Street
Tunbridge Wells
TN3 9DT
Tel: 01892 750101

No. Twelve Queen Street
12 Queen Street
Avon BA1 1NE
Tel: 01225 462363

Partington's Ltd
281 Talbot Road
Manchester M32 0YA
Tel: 0161 928 3616

Payton Interiors
Bretts Farm
Chelmsford Road
White Roding
Essex CM6 1RF
Tel: 01279 876867

Rossiters of Bath
38–41 Broad Street
Bath BA1 5LP
Tel: 01225 462227

Sandra Jane Ltd
46–48 King Street
Cambridge CB1 1LN
Tel: 01223 323211

Woodstock Designs
7 High Street
Woodstock
Oxfordshire OX20 1TE
Tel: 01993 811887

PAINTS

Farrow and Ball
Uddens Trading Estate,
Wimborne
Dorset BH21 7NL
For stockists call 01202 876 141
Produces the National Trust range of colours

Jane Churchill Ltd
See entry for Main Showroom on this page; also by mail order from Farrow and Ball (see above)

Papers and Paints
4 Park Walk, London SW10
Tel: 020 7352 8626
Specialist paints

Sanderson Paints
For stockists call 01895 238 244

CARPETS, RUGS AND FLOORING

Christopher Farr
212 Westbourne Grove
London W11 2RH
020 7792 5761

Crucial Trading
PO Box 11
Duke Place
Kidderminster
Worcestershire DY10 2JR
Tel: 01562 825656

Habitat
196 Tottenham Court Road
London W1P 9LD
020 7631 3880
And branches nationwide

IKEA
Brent Park
2 Drury Way
North Circular Road
London NW10 0TH
Tel: 020 8208 5600
And branches nationwide

Roger Oates
1 Munro Terrace,
Cheyne Walk
London SW10 0DL
Tel: 020 7351 2288

Sinclair Till
791–793 Wandsworth Bridge Road
London SW8 3JQ
Tel: 020 7720 0031

Wool Classics
41 Ledbury Road
London W11 2AA
Tel: 020 7792 8277

FURNITURE

The Conran Shop
Michelin Building
81 Fulham Road
London SW3 6RD
Tel: 020 7589 7401

The Dining Chair Company
4 St Barnabus Street
London SW1W 8PE
Tel: 020 7259 0422

The Dining Room Shop
62–64 Whitehart Lane
Barnes SW13 0PZ
Tel: 020 8878 1020

Grand Illusions
2/4 Crown Road
St Margarets
Twickenham TW1 3EE
Tel: 020 8607 9446

Habitat
See under 'Carpets, Rugs and Flooring'

Heal's
196 Tottenham Court Road
London W1P 9LD
0207 636 1666

IKEA
See under 'Carpets, Rugs and Flooring'

Jane Churchill Ltd
See under 'Main Showroom'

John Lewis
See under 'Department Stores'

Kingcome Sofas
304 Fulham Road
London SW10 9EP
Tel: 020 7351 3998

The Pier
200 Tottenham Court Road
London W1
Tel: 020 7637 7001
And branches nationwide

Sofa Workshop
84 Tottenham Court Road
London W1
Tel: 0207 580 6839
And branches nationwide

Yeoward South
Space S
The Old Imperial Laundry
71 Warriner Gardens
London SW11 4XW
Tel: 020 7351 5454

BED LINEN

Cologne and Cotton
791 Fulham Road
London SW6
Tel: 020 7736 9261
Peacock Blue
201 New Kings Road
London SW6 4SR
Tel: 020 77384 3400

The White Company
189 Munster Road
London SW6 6AW
Tel: 020 7385 7988

CURTAIN POLES AND BLINDS

Artisan
Unit 4a Union Court,
20 Union Road,
London SW4 6JP
Tel: 020 7627 1759

Blue Door
74 Church Road
Barnes
SW13
Tel: 020 8748 9785

The Bradley Collection
Lion Barn
Maitland Road
Needham Market
Suffolk IP6 8NS
Tel: 01449 722728

Byron & Byron
4 Hanover Yard,
London N7 2UH
Tel: 020 8510 4800

John Lewis
See under 'Department Stores'

McKinney & Co
The Old Imperial Laundry
71 Warriner Gardens
London SW11 4XW
Tel: 020 7627 5077

LIGHTING

Habitat
See under 'Carpets, Rugs and Flooring'

Heals
See under 'Furniture'

Hector Finch
88–90 Wandsworth Bridge Road
London SW6 2TF
Tel:020 7731 8886

IKEA
See under 'Carpets and Flooring'

Mr Light
279 King's Road
London SW3 5EW

Tel: 020 7352 8398
Inhouse
24–26 Wilson Street
Glasgow G1 1SS
Tel: 0141 552 5902

Jane Churchill Ltd
See under 'Main Showroom'

John Cullen Lighting
585 King's Road
London SW6 2EH
Tel: 020 7371 5400

John Lewis
See under 'Department Stores'

ACCESSORIES

Beside the Waves
10 Arwenack Street
Falmouth
Cornwall TR11 3JA
Tel: 01326 211132
Paintings and ceramics

Bridgewater
739 Fulham Road
London SW6 5UL
0207 371 5264
Hand-made pottery

Caroline Zoob at Housepoints
48 Webb's Road
London SW11 6NF
Tel: 020 7978 6445
Specialist textiles

The Conran Shop
See under 'Furniture'

Decorative Living
55 New Kings Road
London SW6 4SE
Tel: 020 7736 5623

De Le Cuona Ltd
9/10 Osborne Mews
Windsor
Berkshire SL4 3DE
Tel: 01753 830 301
Cushions and throws

Dining Room Shop
See under 'Furniture'

Divertimenti
139–141 Fulham Road
London SW3 6SD
Tel: 020 7581 8065
Tableware

Habitat
See under 'Furniture'

The Mariners Supply Company
22 Avenue Road
Falmouth
Cornwall TR11 4AZ
Tel: 01326 318841

Pimpernel & Partners
596 Kings Road
London SW6 2DX
Tel: 020 7731 2448

V.V. Rouleaux
54 Sloane Square
Cliveden Place
London SW1W 8AX
Tel: 020 7730 3125
Trims and ribbons

ANTIQUES

Alfie's Antiques Market
13–25 Church Street
London NW8 8DT
Tel: 020 7723 6066

Josephine Ryan Antiques
63 Abbeville Road
London SW14 9JW
Tel: 020 8675 3900

Joss Graham
10 Eccleston Street
London SW1W 9LT
Tel: 020 7730 4370

Judy Greenwood
657 Fulham Road
London SW6 5PY
Tel: 020 7736 6037

Lots Road Auction Galleries
71–73 Lots Road
Chelsea SW10
Tel: 020 7351 7771

Mark Maynard
651 Fulham Road
London SW6 5PU
Tel: 020 7731 3533

Richard Scott Antiques
30 High Street
Holt
Norfolk NR25 6BH
Antique ceramics

Robert Stephenson
1 Elyston Street
Chelsea Green
London SW3 3NT
Tel: 020 7225 2343
Antique rugs

Tobias and the Angel
68 Whitehart Lane
Barnes SW13 0PZ
Tel: 020 8878 8902

FLOWERS AND PLANTS

Chelsea Gardener
125 Sydney Street
London SW3
Tel: 0207 352 5656
Plants, pots, furniture

Columbia Rd Flower Market
London EC2 (Bethnal Green tube)
Every Sunday; good-value plants and cut flowers

Langley Boxwood Nursery
Rake, Liss
Hampshire GU33 7JL
Tel: 01730 894467
Specializes in box topiary

FLORISTS

Paula Pryke
20 Penton St
London N1
Tel: 020 7837 7336

Stephen Woodhams
Woodhams at One Aldwych
London WC2 4BZ
Tel: 020 7300 0777

Wild at Heart
222 Westbourne Grove,
London W11 POST CODE
Tel: 020 7727 3095

ARCHITECTS, DECORATORS AND DESIGNERS

Royal Institute of British Architects
66 Portland Place
London W1B 1AD
Tel: 020 7580 5533
Publishes a list of members

Interior Decorators and Designers
Association
1-4 Chelsea Harbour and Design
Centre
Chelsea Harbour
London SW10 0XE
Tel: 020 7349 0800
Publishes a list of members

MAJOR JANE CHURCHILL STOCKISTS WORLDWIDE

AUSTRALIA
Geraldine Cooper Australia Pty Ltd
255 Burwood Road
Hawthorn, Victoria 3122
Tel: (61) 03 9818 3122

BELGIUM/LUXEMBOURG
Societe Sogestis
90a rue du Page
1050 Brussels
Tel: (32) 2534 5172

CANADA
Primavera Interiors
160 Pears Avenue, Ste. 110
Toronto, Ontario M5R 1T2
Tel : (1) 416 921 3334

FINLAND
Oy SW Lauritzon & Co AB
Hameentie 111
00550 Helsinki
Tel: (358) 9 777 1800

FRANCE
Jane Churchill
7 rue de Furstenberg
75006 Paris
Tel: (33) 1 40 51 95 30

GERMANY/AUSTRIA/SWITZERLAND
Colefax and Fowler GmbH
Georgenstrasse 34
80799 Munich
Tel: (49) 89 339 9720

GREECE
Eurotextile
7a Fokylidou Street
Kolonaki
106 73 Athens
Tel: (30) 1 3632 760

HONG KONG
Mercer House Interiors Ltd
Ground Floor, Wilson House
19-27 Wyndham Street
Central, Hong Kong
Tel: (852) 2524 2000

ITALY
Colefax and Fowler Srl
Via Mario Pagano 12
20145 Milan
Tel: (39) 02 3493 2080

JAPAN
Tomita Textiles
3-16 Kyobashi
2 Chome, Chuo-Ku
Tokyo 104
Tel: (81) 3 3273 7555

THE NETHERLANDS
Suzanne Testa
Waldeck Pyrmont Laan 22A
3743 De Baarn
Tel: (31) 35 541 1749

NEW ZEALAND
Atelier Textile
55 Boston Road, Wellesley Street
Mount Eden
Auckland
Tel: (64) 9 373 3866

NORWAY
Poesi Interioragentur AS
Erling Skjalgssonsgt. 19A
0267 Oslo
Tel: (47) 22 12 81 80

SOUTH AFRICA
Mavromac
12D Kramer Road, Kramerville
Johannesburg 2144
Tel: (27) 11 444 1584

SPAIN
Gaston y. Daniela
Hermosilla 26
28001 Madrid
Tel: (34) 91 485 2590

SWEDEN
Cadoro Agenturer AB
Nybrogatan 77
114 40 Stockholm
Tel: (46) 8 660 2346

TURKEY
Imrahor
Faik Pasa sk. No 9/1
Cukurcuma Taskim
Istanbul
Tel: (90) 212 243 2700

USA

Arizona
Dean-Warren Ltd
Arizona Design Center
2716 N. 68th Street, Ste. 4000
Scottsdale, AZ 85257
Tel: (1) 480 990 9233

California
Cowtan & Tout
2 Henry Adams Street
San Francisco, CA 94103
Tel: (1) 415 863 3955

Oakmont
8687 Melrose Avenue, Ste. B647
Los Angeles, CA 90069
Tel: (1) 310 659 1423

Colorado
Egg & Dart Ltd
595 South Broadway, Ste. 105W
Denver, CO 80209
Tel: (1) 303 744 1676

District of Columbia
Hines & Co
300 'D' Street SW, Ste. 310
Washington, DC 20024
Tel: (1) 202 484 8200

Florida
Nessen Showroom
1855 Griffin Road, Ste. B260
Dania, FL 33004
Tel: (1) 954 925 0606

Georgia
Travis & Co
351 Peachtree Hills Avenue NE, Ste.
128
Atlanta, GA 30305
Tel: (1) 404 237 5079

Illinois
Cowtan & Tout
638 Merchandise Mart
Chicago, IL 60654
Tel: (1) 312 644 0717

Massachusetts
The Martin Group
One Design Center Place, Ste. 111
Boston, MA 02210
Tel: (1) 617 951 2526

Michigan
Rozmallin
1700 Stutz Drive, Ste. 60
Troy, MI 48084
Tel: 248 643 8828

New York
Cowtan & Tout
979 Third Avenue, Ste. 1022, Ste 1005
New York, NY 10022
Tel: (1) 212 753 4488

Oregon
Wayne Martin Inc.
210 Northwest 21st Street
Portland, OR 97209
Tel: (1) 503 221 1555

Philadelphia
Croce Inc.
The Market Place
2400 Market Street, Ste. 218
Philadelphia, PA 19103
Tel: (1) 215 561 6160

Texas
Walter Lee Culp Associates
Dallas Design Center
1025 North Stemmons Freeway, Ste.
500
Dallas, Tx 75207
Tel: (1) 214 651 0510
and at:
5120 Woodway Drive, Ste. 4018
Houston, TX 77056
Tel: (1) 713 623 4670

Utah
Egg & Dart Ltd.
741 South 400 West, Ste. 200
Salt Lake City, UT 84101
Tel: (1) 801 533 9119

Washington
Wayne Martin Inc.
1000 Lenora Street, Ste. 200
Seattle, WA 98121
Tel: (1) 206 224 7171

Index

Numbers in italics refer to illustration captions.

Acknowledgements

I would like to thank those who so kindly allowed us to use their homes for photography: Mr and Mrs Nicholas Arbuthnot, Trudi Ballard, Madame Simone Dumont, Laura George, Mr and Mrs Richard Leonard, Michael Lock, Lynn Morgan, Emma Price, Megan de Roulet, Ali Sharland and Maddy Thornhill.

A huge thank you to the following people who offered their enormous talent, help and support to this project: everyone at Jane Churchill and especially Trudi Ballard, Lizzie McClatchie, Emma Price, Helen McKay and Benedicte Parent de Lannoy. I am also grateful to Sarnia Ketcher and Jeannie Moore, David Rowe and his team, Gerry Kennelly, Ann Manzy, Victor Bishop, Richard Tuff, Kingcome sofas, and all the other people behind the scenes, far too numerous to list, who made such a valuable contribution.

Thanks must go to my publisher, Jacqui Small, and to those who were involved with the production of the book: Helen Chislett, Stuart Cooper, Mary Norden, Robin Rout, Simon Upton and Sam Walsh. They were all magnificent.

I would like to express my appreciation to David Green for his support and to Michael Lock for his wonderful creative talent, inspiration and friendship throughout my career with Jane Churchill, and to Sarah Charles and Andy Luckett for their invaluable support over the years.

Finally, I am very grateful to my friends for their support and cheerful acceptance of my incredibly busy schedule, and to my family: Roy, my husband, and Tom and Lottie, my children, for their love and encouragement.